Silly Salamanders
and Other Slightly Stupid Stuff
for Readers Theatre

Anthony D. Fredericks

Illustrated by
Anthony A. Stoner

2000
Teacher Ideas Press
Libraries Unlimited
A Division of Greenwood Publishing Group, Inc.
Englewood, Colorado

TEACHER IDEAS PRESS
Libraries Unlimited
A Division of Greenwood Publishing Group, Inc.
P.O. Box 6633
Englewood, CO 80155-6633
1-800-237-6124
www.lu.com/tip

Library of Congress Cataloging-in-Publication Data

Fredericks, Anthony D.
    Silly salamanders and other slightly stupid stuff for readers theatre / Anthony D. Fredericks
      p. cm.
    Includes bibliographical references.
    ISBN 1-56308-825-8
    1. Readers' theater. 2. Fairy tales--Parodies, imitations, etc. I. Title.

PN2081.R4 F747 2000
372.67'6--dc21

00-060777

Silly Salamanders and Other Slightly Stupid Stuff for Readers Theatre

Dedicated to my very best friend _____

Who is one of the most creative, dynamic,
and exciting teachers on the entire planet!
(Thanks, I couldn't have done it without you!)

Contents

Part I
The Part That Comes Near the Beginning
of the Book

Part II
A Whole Bunch of Wild and Wacky Scripts That Will Make Your Students
Think You Are the Coolest Teacher Who Ever Lived!

Part III
Oh Boy, Oh Boy, a Bunch of Stories About Salamanders

Part IV
The Part of the Book That Is Pretty Close
to the End of the Book

Part V
This Is the Appendix Part of the Book or the Section Where Those "Brand X"
Authors Put Lots of Dumb Stuff so That Their Books Look a Lot Bigger Than They
Really Are—but in This Book the Stuff Here Is Really Neat (Trust Me)

Acknowledgments

The creation of this book was encouraged by friends, advocated by colleagues, influenced by teachers, motivated by librarians; and, of course, inspired by salamanders everywhere.

To the readers of *Frantic Frogs and Other Frankly Fractured Folktales for Readers Theatre* and *Tadpole Tales and Other Totally Terrific Treats for Readers Theatre*, I extend my heartfelt thanks and everlasting appreciation for all your letters, notes, e-mails, and personal contacts at numerous workshops and conferences. Your unfailing support and sincere enthusiasm for readers theatre as a valuable and viable language arts technique was a powerful stimulant and perpetual catalyst for the creation of this third book in the trilogy.

To King Arthur and his knights, who let me stay at the castle while conducting my research on the halitosis-plagued (and less than fiery) dragon, thanks a million.

To Mother Goose, who continues to supply me with an endless procession of delightful characters and engaging story possibilities (but for whom I've never written an individual story), goes a thunderous round of applause.

To Goldilocks, who allowed me to write about another incident in her life (although I was legally prevented from mentioning the "breaking and entering" episode at the cottage in the woods), I extend my sincere appreciation.

To both Beauty and The Beast, who give new meaning to the term "opposites attract," goes a hearty "thank you."

A warm note of recognition goes to all the witches, giants, trolls, evil stepmothers, wizards, and other outcasts in Storybookland who never seem to get the literary credit they deserve.

To Ms. White and her seven vertically challenged friends goes a great big tip of the hat for that wild and crazy sing-along down at the cabin. (Oh, by the way, did anyone notice what happened to the basket of apples by the front door?)

To Hansel and Gretel, who are frequently portrayed as parentally deprived, crumb-following, sucrose-ingesting, and witch-burning misfits, go my best wishes for success in your new lives.

Mia Semuta Preneau, my Webmaster, whose creativity and dedication in designing a truly magical Web site (http://www.afredericks.com) for elementary teachers, is to be honored and celebrated.

And, most especially, to kids everywhere whose silliness is the inspiration for these stories, whose craziness is the eternal elixir for one somewhat balding author, whose wackiness fills classrooms with ceaseless laughter, and whose enthusiasm makes teaching such a constant joy, go my unwavering gratitude and admiration.

This Section of the Book Is Known As "THE PREFACE" and It Is Frequently a Collection of Leftover Thoughts That the Author Didn't Know What to Do with—Except in This Case, Where It Is Actually a True Story (Well, Sort of) About How This Book Came to Be

SOMEWHAT BALDING AUTHOR: Gosh, I have entirely too much time on my hands. All I do is teach a bunch of classes every day, grade papers, plan lessons, develop new units, meet with students, give tests, and then do a couple of chores on the "honey-do" list my wife gives me each week.

GREAT AND MAGNIFICENT EDITOR: Well, you know, Somewhat Balding Author, you could write another readers theatre book.

SOMEWHAT BALDING AUTHOR: Gosh, do you really think so?

GREAT AND MAGNIFICENT EDITOR: You bet! Remember how successful *Frantic Frogs and Other Frankly Fractured Folktales for Readers Theatre* was when it came out? Fourth- to eighth-grade teachers all over the country were clamoring for copies of that resource.

SOMEWHAT BALDING AUTHOR: Yeah, that's right. I got tons of letters from teachers all over the country saying how much they liked that book. In fact, I'm still getting letters. By the way, what does the word "clamoring" mean?

WONDERFUL AND DELIGHTFUL TEACHER: Yes, that book was one of the most brilliant and creative teacher resources I've ever used with my students. They couldn't stop laughing for weeks.

SOMEWHAT BALDING AUTHOR: Gee, thanks Wonderful and Delightful Teacher. Say, by the way, how did you get into this phone conversation with Great and Magnificent Editor and me?

WONDERFUL AND DELIGHTFUL TEACHER: That's just one of the miracles of modern communication.

GREAT AND MAGNIFICENT EDITOR: And then a few years later you wrote that marvelous book, *Tadpole Tales and Other Totally Terrific Treats for Readers Theatre.* As you know, that book was designed for teachers of grades one through four. And, boy, did that book take off like a bat out of #$%&!

CREATIVE AND DYNAMIC TEACHER: You bet, I simply loved using all those scripts with my students. It was one of the best things I ever did for my language arts program. Kids were falling all over themselves with giggles and laughter.

SOMEWHAT BALDING AUTHOR: Hey, how did we get another person in on this conversation? When did this become a party line?

SUAVE AND DEBONAIR TEACHER: Don't you never mind! We just think that those two books have made a world of difference in our classrooms—they're fresh, engaging, and full of fun!

SOMEWHAT BALDING AUTHOR: Well, gosh, thanks a lot! Is there anyone else who would like to get into this conversation?

PROSPECTIVE TEACHER OF THE YEAR: Yes, indeed! I think it's about time you sat down and wrote another readers theatre book—another one filled with grins, giggles, and guffaws just like the other two.

GREAT AND MAGNIFICENT EDITOR: That's right, Somewhat Balding Author! We've received lots and lots of requests from teachers all over the country for another readers theatre book. They can't seem to get enough of your wild and wacky humor.

PROSPECTIVE TEACHER OF THE YEAR: Yes, we just think your books are the best ever!

SOMEWHAT BALDING AUTHOR: Of course, everyone reading this will know that I just made up that previous comment myself.

GREAT AND MAGNIFICENT EDITOR: Nevertheless, we here at Teacher Ideas Press think that your books are the best ever! We would like to offer you a contract with tons and tons of money.

SOMEWHAT BALDING AUTHOR: Of course, everyone reading this will know that I just made up that previous comment myself (again).

SUAVE AND DEBONAIR TEACHER: So, what do you say, Somewhat Balding Author? Will you p-l-e-a-s-e, p-l-e-a-s-e, p-l-e-a-s-e write another readers theatre book?

CREATIVE AND DYNAMIC TEACHER: Yes, and I think I've even got a possible title for the book. How about *Silly Salamanders and Other Slightly Stupid Stuff for Readers Theatre*?

SOMEWHAT BALDING AUTHOR: Wow, that's a great idea. I guess that's why you're known as Creative and Dynamic Teacher.

WONDERFUL AND DELIGHTFUL TEACHER: And I think that the types of stories in the book should be fables, legends, folktales, myths, and "other."

SOMEWHAT BALDING AUTHOR: Hey, these are super ideas. I guess I better start working on this new book so that teachers can begin using the readers theatre scripts in their classrooms right away.

GREAT AND MAGNIFICENT EDITOR: WOW! I'm delighted. While you're writing more hilarious readers theatre scripts, let me write you a big fat check. And, by the way, would you like a BMW and a condo in Hawaii included in your contract, too?

INNOCENT BYSTANDER: And so it was. Somewhat Balding Author wrote the book you now hold in your hands. Great and Magnificent Editor wrote an enormous check and gave Somewhat Balding Author a brand new BMW. Wonderful and Delightful Teacher, Creative and Dynamic Teacher, Suave and Debonair Teacher, Prospective Teacher of the Year, and thousands of educators around the country purchased copies of this book. Students all over laughed and chuckled for weeks and months. Schools in every state were filled with mirth and merriment. And they all lived happily ever after.

Part I

THE PART THAT COMES NEAR THE BEGINNING OF THE BOOK

O.K., This Is the Really Serious Stuff in the Book That You Should Read Before You Read All the Incredibly Humorous Stuff in the Rest of the Book

The Magic of Storytelling

Not too long ago a colleague asked me what I enjoyed most about teaching youngsters. My response was immediate and emphatic—storytelling! To watch the gleam of excitement in students' eyes while sharing a new book, to observe the look of recognition when presenting a familiar tale, or to see kids' faces light up when embellishing a piece of literature or timeless tale are professional "perks" that go far beyond paychecks and long vacations. I suppose part of my belief that storytelling is the quintessential classroom activity lies in the fact that it is an opportunity to bring life, vitality, and substance to the two-dimensional letters and words on a printed page. So, too, is it an interpersonal activity—a "no-fail" way to connect with minds and souls and hearts. After more than 30 years of teaching, I never tire of sharing a story with a group of youngsters—it is part of my *raison d'être* as I hope it will be for them.

The magic of storytelling has been a tradition of every culture and civilization since the dawn of language. It binds human beings and celebrates their heritage as no other language art can. It is part and parcel of the human experience because it underscores the values and experiences we cherish as well as those we seek to share with each other. Nowhere is this more important than in today's classroom. Young children, who have been bombarded with visual messages (i.e., televisions and computers) since birth, still relish and appreciate the power and majesty of a story well told. Even adults, with their hustle and bustle lifestyles, enjoy the magic of a story or the enchantment of a storyteller. Perhaps it is a natural part of who we are that stories command our attention and help us appreciate the values, ideas, and traditions we hold dear. So, too, should children have those same experiences and those same pleasures.

Storytelling conjures up all sorts of visions and possibilities: far-away lands, magnificent adventures, enchanted princes, beautiful princesses, evil wizards and wicked witches, a few dragons and demons, a couple of castles and cottages, perhaps a mysterious forest or two, and certainly tales of mystery, intrigue, and adventure. These are stories of tradition and timelessness, tales that enchant, mystify, and excite through a marvelous weaving of characters, settings, and plots, . . .tales that have stood the test of time. They are stories of our youth, stories of our heritage, and stories that continue to enrapture audiences with their delightful blending of good over evil, patience over greed, and right over might. Our senses are stimulated, our mental images are energized, and our experiences are fortified through the magic of storytelling.

What Is Readers Theatre?

Readers theatre is a storytelling device that stimulates the imagination and promotes *all* of the language arts. Simply stated, it is an oral interpretation of a piece of literature read in a dramatic style. My good friend, Suzanne Barchers—who is also an author of several readers theatre books (see Appendix C)—states that, ". . . the primary focus in readers theatre is on an effective reading of the script rather than on a . . . memorized presentation. . . . The ease of incorporating readers theatre into the language arts program offers teachers an exciting way to enhance that program, especially in today's classrooms that emphasize a variety of reading and listening experiences." (Barchers, 1993).

Simply put, readers theatre is an act of involvement, an opportunity to share, a time to creatively interact with others, and a personal interpretation of what can be or could be. Readers theatre holds the promise of helping children to understand and appreciate the richness of language, the interpretation of that language, and how language can be a powerful vehicle for the comprehension and appreciation of different forms of literature. It provides numerous opportunities for youngsters to make stories and literature come alive and pulsate with their own unique brand of perception and vision. In so doing, literature becomes personal and reflective, and children have a breadth of opportunities to be authentic users of language.

Students As Storytellers

One of the positive consequences of having regular storytelling times in the classroom is that children begin to understand that storytelling is a natural act of communication. Witness the excitement of primary level students returning from a trip or holiday vacation as they eagerly share their stories with the teacher or other members of the class. Here, the energy level is at an all-time high as family episodes, tales, and personal experiences are shared back and forth. Indeed, youngsters soon learn that we are all storytellers, all with something to share.

When children are provided with regular opportunities in the classroom to become storytellers, they develop a personal stake in the literature shared. They also begin to cultivate personal interpretations of that literature—interpretations that lead to higher levels of appreciation and comprehension. Practicing and performing stories is an involvement endeavor, one that demonstrates and utilizes numerous languaging activities. Youngsters learn to listen to their classmates and appreciate a variety of presentations.

What Is the Value of Readers Theatre?

I like to think of readers theatre as a way to interpret literature without the constraints of skills, memorization, or artificial structures (e.g., props, costumes, elaborate staging). Readers theatre allows children to breathe life and substance into literature. Their interpretation is neither right nor wrong because it will be colored by kids' unique perspectives, experiences, and vision. In fact, the readers' interpretation of a story is intrinsically more valuable than some predetermined and/or preordained "translation" (something that might be found in a teacher's manual or curriculum guide, for example).

With that in mind, I'd like to share with you some of the many values I see in readers theatre:

- It stimulates curiosity and enthusiasm for different forms of literature. It allows children to experiences stories in a supportive and nonthreatening format that underscores their active involvement.

- Because readers theatre allows children many different interpretations of the same story, it facilitates the development of critical and creative thinking. There is no such thing as a right or wrong interpretation of a story, and . . . readers theatre validates that assumption.

- Readers theatre focuses on all of the language arts: reading, writing, speaking, and listening. It supports a holistic philosophy of instruction and allows children to become responsible learners, ones who seek out answers to their own self-initiated inquiries.

- Because it is the performance that drives readers theatre, children are given more opportunities to invest themselves and their personalities in the production. The same story may be subject to several different presentations depending on the group or the individual youngsters involved. Children learn that readers theatre (just like other forms of literature) can be explored in a host of ways and a host of possibilities.

- Children are given numerous opportunities to learn about the major features of children's literature: plot, theme, setting, point of view, and characterization. This is particularly true when they are provided with opportunities to design and construct their own readers theatre scripts and have unlimited opportunities to discover the wide variations that can be used with a single piece.

- Readers theatre is a participatory event. The characters as well as the audience are all intimately involved in the design, structure, and delivery of the story. As a result, children begin to realize that reading is not a solitary activity but rather one that can be shared and discussed with others.

- Readers theatre is informal and relaxed. It does not require elaborate props, scenery, or costumes. It can be set up in any classroom or library. It does not require large sums of money to "make it happen," and it can be "put on" in any kind of environment, formal or informal.

- Readers theatre stimulates the imagination and the creation of visual images. It has been substantiated that when youngsters are provided with opportunities to create their own mental images, their comprehension and appreciation of a piece of writing will be enhanced considerably. Because only a modicum of formal props and "set up" are required for any readers theatre production, the participants and audience are encouraged to create supplemental "props" in their minds, props that may be more elaborate and exquisite than those found in the most lavish of plays.

- Readers theatre enhances the development of cooperative learning strategies by requiring youngsters to work together toward a common goal and supporting their efforts to do so. Readers theatre is not a competitive activity, but rather a cooperative one in which children share, discuss, and band together for the good of the production.

- Readers theatre is valuable for non-English-speaking children or nonfluent readers. It provides them with positive models of language usage and interpretation that extend far beyond the "decoding" of printed materials. It allows them to see "language in action" and the various ways in which language can be used.

- Teachers and librarians have also discovered that readers theatre is an excellent way in which to enhance the development of communication skills. Voice projection, intonation, inflection, and pronunciation skills are all promoted within and throughout any readers theatre production. Children who need assistance in these areas are provided with a support structure that encourages the development of necessary abilities.

- The development and enhancement of self-concept is facilitated through readers theatre. Because children are working in concert with other children in a supportive atmosphere, their self-esteem mushrooms accordingly. Again, the emphasis is on the presentation, not necessarily the performers. Youngsters have opportunities to develop levels of self-confidence and self-assurance that would not normally be available in more traditional class productions.

- Creative and critical thinking are enhanced through the utilization of readers theatre. Children are active participants in the interpretation and delivery of a story; they develop thinking skills that are divergent rather than convergent, and interpretive skills that are supported rather than directed.

- When children are provided with opportunities to write and/or script their own readers theatre, their writing abilities are supported and encouraged. As children become familiar with the design and format of readers theatre scripts they can begin to utilize their creative talents in designing their own scripts and stories.

- Readers theatre is fun! Children of all ages have delighted in using readers theatre for many years. It is delightful and stimulating, encouraging and fascinating, relevant and personal. Indeed, try as I might, I have not been able to locate a single instance (or group of children) in which (or for whom) readers theatre would not be an appropriate language arts activity. It is a strategy filled with a cornucopia of possibilities and promises.

Presentation Suggestions

It is important to remember that there is no single way to present readers theatre. What follows are some ideas you and the youngsters with whom you work may wish to keep in mind as you put on the productions in this book. Different classes and even different groups of children within the same class will each have their own method and mode of presentation; in other words, no two presentations may ever be the same. However, following are some suggestions that will help make any readers theatre performance successful.

Preparing Scripts

One of the advantages of using readers theatre in the classroom is the lack of extra work or preparation time necessary to get "up and running." If you use the scripts in this book, your preparation time will be minimal.

- After a script has been selected for presentation, make sufficient copies. A copy of the script should be provided for each actor. Also make two or three extra copies, one for you and "replacement" copies for scripts that are accidentally damaged or lost. Copies for the audience are unnecessary and are not suggested.

- Bind each script between two sheets of colored construction paper or in a colored folder. Bound scripts tend to formalize the presentation and lend an air of professionalism to the actors.

- Highlight each character's speaking parts with different color highlighter pens. This helps youngsters track their parts without being distracted by the dialogue of others.

Starting Out

Introducing the concept of readers theatre to your students for the first time may be as simple as sharing a script with the entire class and "walking" youngsters through the design and delivery of that script.

- Emphasize that a readers theatre performance does not require any memorization of the script. It's the interpretation and performance that count.

- Read through an entire script aloud, taking on the various roles. Let students see how easy and comfortable this process is.

- Encourage selected volunteers to read assigned parts of a sample script to the entire class. Readers should stand or sit in a circle so that other classmates can observe them.

- Provide opportunities for additional re-readings using other volunteers. Plan time to discuss the ease of presentation and the different interpretations offered by different readers.

- Give readers an opportunity to practice their scripts before presenting them to an audience. Take some time to discuss voice intonation, facial gestures, body movements, and other features that could be used to enhance the presentation.

- Allow children the opportunity to suggest their own modifications, adaptations, or interpretations of the script. They will undoubtedly be "in tune" with the interests and perceptions of their peers and can offer some distinctive and personal interpretations.

- Encourage students to select nonstereotypical roles within any readers theatre script. For example, boys can take on female roles and girls can take on male roles, the smallest person in the class can take on the role of a giant, or a shy student can take on the role of a boastful, bragging character. Provide sufficient opportunities for students to expand and extend their appreciation of readers theatre through a variety of "out of character" roles.

Staging

Staging involves the physical location of the readers as well as any necessary movements. Unlike a more formal play, in readers theatre the movements are often minimal. The emphasis is more on presentation; less on action.

- For most presentations readers will stand and/or sit on stools or chairs. The physical location of each reader has been indicated for each of the scripts in this book.

- The position of each reader is determined by "power of character" (Dixon et al., 1996). This means that the main character is down-stage center (in the middle front of the staging area) and the lesser characters are stage right, stage left, or farther upstage (toward the rear of the staging area).

- If there are many characters in the presentation, it may be advantageous to have characters in the rear (upstage) standing while those in the front (downstage) are placed on stools or chairs. This ensures that the audience will both see and hear each actor.

- Usually all of the characters will be on stage throughout the duration of the presentation. For most presentations it is not necessary to have characters enter and exit. If you place the characters on stools, they can face the audience when they are involved in a particular scene and then turn around whenever they are not involved.

- You may wish to make simple, hand-lettered signs with the name of each character. Loop a piece of string or yarn through each sign and hang it around the neck of that character. In this way the audience will know the identity of each character throughout the presentation.

- Slightly more formalized presentations will have various characters entering and exiting at various times throughout the presentation. These directions are indicated in the scripts in this book.

- Each reader will have his or her own copy of the script in a paper cover (see above). If possible, use a music stand for each reader's script. (This allows readers to use their hands for dramatic interpretations as necessary.)

- Several presentations have a narrator to set up the story. The narrator serves to establish the place and time of the story for the audience so that the characters can "jump into" their parts from the beginning of the story. Typically, the narrator is separated from the other "actors" and can be identified by a simple sign.

- As students become more comfortable with readers theatre, invite them to suggest alternative positions for characters in a script. The placements indicated in these scripts are only suggestions; students may want to "experiment" with various staging possibilities. This becomes a worthwhile cooperative activity and demonstrates the variety of interpretations possible with any single script.

Props

Two of the positive features of readers theatre are its ease of preparation and its ease of presentation. Informality is a hallmark of any readers theatre script.

- Much of the setting for a story should take place in the audience's mind. Elaborate scenery is not necessary—simple props are often the best. For example:

  - A branch or potted plant can serve as a tree.

  - A drawing on the chalkboard can illustrate a building.

  - A hand-lettered sign can designate one part of the staging area as a particular scene (e.g., swamp, castle, field, forest).

  - Children's toys can be used for uncomplicated props (e.g., telephone, vehicles).

  - A sheet of aluminum foil or a remnant of blue cloth can be used to simulate a lake or pond.

- Costumes for the actors are unnecessary. A few simple items may be suggested by students. For example:

  - Hats, scarves, or aprons can be used by major characters.

  - A paper cutout can serve as a tie, button, or badge.

  - Old clothing (borrowed from parents) can be used as applicable.

- Some teachers and librarians have discovered that the addition of appropriate music or sound effects can enhance a readers theatre presentation. For example, the beat of a drum for the giant in "Jack and the Beanstalk," a classical waltz for the scene at the ball in "Cinderella," or the ticking of a clock in "Hickory, Dickory Dock . . . " all add to the story.

- It's important to remember that the emphasis in readers theatre is on the reading, not on any accompanying "features." The best presentations are often the simplest.

Delivery

I've often found it advantageous to let students know that the only difference between a readers theatre presentation and a movie role is the fact that they will have a script in their hands. This allows them to focus more on presenting a script rather than on memorizing it.

- When first introduced to readers theatre, students often have a tendency to "read into" their scripts. Encourage students to look up from their scripts and interact with other characters or the audience as necessary.

- Practicing the script beforehand can eliminate the problem of students burying their heads in the pages. Children need to understand the importance of involving the audience as much as possible in the development of the story.

- Voice projection and delivery are important in allowing the audience to understand character actions. The proper mood and intent need to be established, which is possible when children are familiar and comfortable with each character's "style."

- Children should not memorize their lines but rather rehearse them sufficiently so that they are "comfortable" with them. Again, the emphasis is on delivery, so be sure to suggest different types of voice (e.g., angry, irritated, calm, frustrated, excited) that children may wish to use for their particular character(s).

Post-Presentation

As a wise author once said, "The play's the thing." So it is with readers theatre. In other words, the mere act of presenting a readers theatre script is complete in and of itself. It is not necessary, or even required, to do any type of formalized evaluation after readers theatre. Once again, the emphasis is on informality. Readers theatre should and can be a pleasurable and stimulating experience for children.

What follows are a few ideas you may want to share with students to provide them with important languaging opportunities that extend and promote all aspects of your language arts or library program.

- After a presentation, discuss with students how the script enhanced or altered the original story (as appropriate).

- Invite students to suggest other characters who could be added to the script.

- Invite students to suggest new or alternate dialogue for various characters.

- Invite students to suggest new or different setting(s) for the script.

- Invite students to talk about their reactions to various characters' expressions, tone of voice, presentations, or dialogues.

- Invite youngsters to suggest any modifications or changes needed in the script.

- Invite each of the "cast" members to maintain a "production log" or reading response log in which he or she records thoughts and perceptions about the presentation. Encourage students to share their logs with other class members.

Presenting a readers theatre script need not be an elaborate or extensive production. As children become more familiar with and polished in using readers theatre they will be able to suggest a multitude of presentation possibilities for future scripts. It is important to help children assume a measure of self-initiated responsibility in the delivery of any readers theatre. Doing this will help ensure their personal engagement and active participation in this most valuable of language arts activities.

It is hoped that you and your students will find an abundance of engaging readers theatre scripts in this book for use in your own classroom, but these scripts should also serve as an impetus for the creation of your own classroom or library scripts. By providing opportunities for your students to begin designing their own readers theatre scripts you will be offering them an exciting new arena for the enhancement of their writing and languaging abilities.

References

Barchers, Suzanne. *Readers Theatre for Beginning Readers*. Englewood, CO: Teacher Ideas Press, 1993.

Dixon, Neill, Anne Davies, and Colleen Politano. *Learning with Readers Theatre: Building Connections*. Winnipeg, Canada: Peguis Publishers, 1996.

Fredericks, Anthony D. *Frantic Frogs and Other Frankly Fractured Folktales for Readers Theatre*. Englewood, CO: Teacher Ideas Press, 1993.

———. *Tadpole Tales and Other Totally Terrific Treats for Readers Theatre*. Englewood, CO: Teacher Ideas Press, 1997.

Part II

A WHOLE BUNCH OF WILD AND WACKY SCRIPTS THAT WILL MAKE YOUR STUDENTS THINK YOU ARE THE COOLEST TEACHER WHO EVER LIVED!

The Fire-Breathing Dragon Finally Uses Mouthwash (and, Boy, What a Difference!)

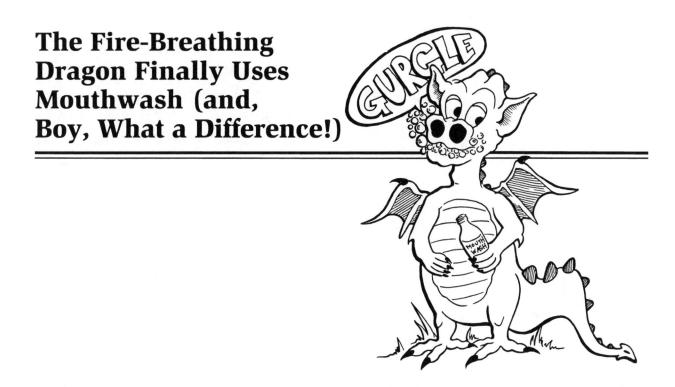

STAGING: The narrator can sit on a stool to the front and side of all the characters. The characters may wish to stand and physically interact with each other or sit in chairs or on stools. Note that the audience has a part in this production, too.

Beautiful Princess   Handsome Prince
X   X

Fire-Breathing Dragon
X

Wise Old Man
X

Narrator
X

NARRATOR: (*apologetically*) Even before we begin this story, I'm going to have to be honest with you. One of the characters behind me is really gross! And I mean GROSS!! He usually shows up in a lot of these "Knights of the Round Table" stories about damsels in distress and handsome knights on white horses who rescue the beautiful young maidens who seem to get into a lot of trouble every time they turn around in the kingdom. But, anyway, I'm getting ahead of myself; because, you see, that character right there (*points to dragon*) has got the world's worst breath. . . . I mean we're talkin' about really gross. In fact, his breath is so bad that he has been banished from the dragon's club and has to live by himself deep in the darkest cave in the kingdom. And that really presents a problem, I mean a major problem, for him. But, maybe I'd better let him tell you his sad tale. And believe me, it's really really sad.

AUDIENCE: AWWWWWWWWWWWWWWWW!

FIRE-BREATHING DRAGON: You see, it's like this. Ever since I got my fire-breathing license I've been wanting to roam the countryside just like all the other fire-breathing dragons and capture my share of fair-haired young maidens and hold them for ransom until some handsome dude on a pale white horse rides up and challenges me to a fight and so on and so on. . . . I think you get the picture.

AUDIENCE: (*emphatically*) OH, YES. WE DO.

FIRE-BREATHING DRAGON: All I wanted to do was to be like all the other dragons—roaming the countryside, capturing young ladies, burning down a couple of forests here and there—you know, the usual dragon stuff. But I had a serious problem that really prevented me from doing my job. (*stammering*) I'm sort of embarrassed to tell you about it, I mean it's not the sort of thing you discuss in polite company, it's, well, you know, I mean . . .

BEAUTIFUL PRINCESS: Let's get it out in the open. What it comes down to is the fact that our friend here (*points to dragon*) has some of the worst-smelling, most offensive, and downright putrid breath in this kingdom or any other kingdom for that matter. I mean, he would get within 50 miles of a castle and everyone would know it—horses would be passing out, trees would be dying by the thousands, all the animals would burrow underground, and you just can't believe what it did to my gorgeous curly blond hair. (*tosses her head and smoothes her hair*)

AUDIENCE:	EWWWWWWWWWW. THAT'S GROSS!
HANDSOME PRINCE:	And, to make matters even worse, all us princes who were out riding around on our wonderful thoroughbred horses looking for ladies to save were being knocked out by the stench of the dragon's breath. We'd ride into the kingdom and be greeted by an odor that turned our horses from white to dark yellow, made our armor rust within 20 seconds, and even made our swords wilt from the aroma. It was beyond the point of gross, it was really sickening.
NARRATOR:	Well, as you might imagine, a couple of things happened. Our friend here (*points to dragon*) couldn't find any decent work. I mean, after all, if you're a fire-breathing dragon your occupation is obviously going to be breathing fire all over the place, raising havoc among the people in the kingdom, scaring poor defenseless young maidens, and making sure that all those wandering knights have something to do with all their free time. But because the dragon couldn't get within seven miles of anybody's castle that meant that the dragon couldn't do the job he was trained for. And a lot of people couldn't do their jobs, either.
AUDIENCE:	AWWWWWWWWW!
WISE OLD MAN:	(*as an aside to the audience*) Right about now, you're probably wondering when I'm going to offer my advice so that this story will have a happy ending. Well, just hang on to your hats, because it's coming up pretty soon.
NARRATOR:	The other thing that happened was that the dragon couldn't go out anywhere. Once he left his cave, people for miles around would know that he was out and they'd all begin putting on their gas masks and hiding in the castle cellar. Nobody was around to greet, or much less fight with, the dragon. The dragon began to feel dejected and began spending more and more of his time in his cave. He didn't come out for long periods of time and that meant that no one had anything to do in stories like this.

AUDIENCE:	AWWWWWWWWWW!
WISE OLD MAN:	(*secretively to audience*) Hold on, my part is coming up real soon, now.
BEAUTIFUL PRINCESS:	It's not that we didn't like him or anything, it's just that . . . well, you know. . . . I mean . . . would you want to have some garlic-breath, halitosis-mouth, liver-tongued creature breathing on you throughout some 300-page story or two-hour movie? Not me . . . no way, José.
FIRE-BREATHING DRAGON:	(*sadly*) Hey, let's face it. I couldn't get a job anywhere. I became withdrawn. I couldn't even live near all my dragon pals. I was banished from one kingdom to another. I was really developing a complex.
AUDIENCE:	AWWWWWWWWW!
HANDSOME PRINCE:	It was really a bad situation. His foul-smelling breath was simply putting a lot of people out of work. Since he retreated to his cave, nobody in any of the stories knew what to do. I mean, after all, this was before Nintendo® and MTV were invented. All we could do was sit around and scratch ourselves.
FIRE-BREATHING DRAGON:	Yeah, it got so bad that I couldn't open my mouth anywhere. I completely lost my desire to burn things down. In fact, after a while I didn't even have enough fire left to cook a meatball. It was bad, really bad!
AUDIENCE:	AWWWWWWWWW!
WISE OLD MAN:	(*very excitedly*) It's coming! It's coming! Listen carefully, my big part is just around the corner. It's almost here! It's almost here!
NARRATOR:	Nobody knew what to do. After all, they really enjoyed having a fire-breathing dragon in the neighborhood, but not one with a breath like old rotting goats. Nobody knew what to do. Then, one day, someone from another story suggested that the dragon go to the top of the mountain and ask the wise old man for any ideas. And so the dragon did.

WISE OLD MAN: (*excitedly*) Yeah, yeah, yeah. F-i-n-a-l-l-y, my big part. That foul-smelling dragon eventually came to me to ask what he should do about his skunky breath. Well, I sat there, pondering his request and stroking my long white beard and staring off into space when, all of a sudden, the answer came to me—MOUTHWASH! That's it, mouthwash. I suggested that he gallop off to the nearest drugstore and get a supply of mouthwash and drink a bottle each and every day. Then, he would be able to do his job and everyone else in the kingdom would be happy, too.

NARRATOR: And that's exactly what happened. The dragon's breath was sparkling clean and kissably fresh. He was able to walk up to a castle without everyone dropping like flies. He was able to snatch beautiful young princesses just like our Beautiful Princess here (*points to Beautiful Princess*) and run off to the forest. And all the handsome young princes just like our Handsome Prince here (*points to Handsome Prince*) were able to keep their jobs saving those damsels in distress. And, the wise old men of the kingdom, just like our Wise Old Man (*points to Wise Old Man*) were celebrated in song and dance. And, as you might imagine, everyone lived happily ever after.

AUDIENCE: (*standing*) HIP HIP HOORAY! HIP HIP HOORAY!! HIP HIP HOORAY!!!

Snow White and the Seven Vertically Challenged Men Who Live in the Forest

STAGING: The narrator should be seated on a tall stool to the side of all the characters. The characters can be standing and moving around throughout the presentation.

```
          Bashful        Dopey        Happy        Grumpy
             X             X             X            X

                    Sneezy         Doc        Sleepy
                       X            X            X

          Snow White
             X

Narrator
   X
```

NARRATOR: Once upon a time, there were . . .

SNOW WHITE: (*angrily*) Now, just wait a minute, buster. Let's get one thing straight. I'm the star of this production, right?

NARRATOR: Yeah, I guess so.

SNOW WHITE: (*in a tough voice*) Hey, you know so. Just so we get things right here let's be clear. I'm the star and so I get top billing. Right?

NARRATOR:	O.K., that's fine with me. But, you see, as the official narrator I must set up the story for the audience out there (*points to audience*).
SNOW WHITE:	That's fine with me, buster. But just don't take up too much of my precious time. In other words, make it quick and make it short.
NARRATOR:	All right, already. Just give me a chance.
SNOW WHITE:	You're on. But I'm watching you!
NARRATOR:	So, as I was saying. . . . Once upon a time, there were seven vertically challenged men who lived in a cabin deep in the forest and who spent their days working in a diamond mine and singing a song called "Hi Ho, Hi Ho, It's Off to Work We Go."
SNOW WHITE:	(*interrupting*) O.K., that's enough. Now it's time for ME.
NARRATOR:	(*as an aside to the audience*) Whew! How did I get linked up with some blonde with an attitude problem?
SNOW WHITE:	Just watch it buster or I'll have your narrator's license pulled.
NARRATOR:	O.K., I'm outta here (*exits offstage*).
SNOW WHITE:	So, let's get on with the story.
SEVEN VERTICALLY CHALLENGED MEN:	(*singing together as they march onstage*) Hi ho, hi ho, it's off to work we go. Hi ho, hi ho, it's off to work we go. Hi ho, hi ho, it's off to . . .
SNOW WHITE:	O.K., guys. You've sung your little song. Now, how about getting into some serious dialogue?
DOC:	Fine, why don't you start things off?

SNOW WHITE:	If you insist. First of all, I'd like to know why you guys all live in this tiny cabin deep in the forest. Couldn't you find a larger place in the suburbs?
SNEEZY:	Well, we tried (*a-CHEW*). But with all seven of us together it was tough finding a place with decent rent (*a-CHEW*). And, besides, have you ever tried looking for a seven-bedroom apartment (*a-CHEW*)?
SNOW WHITE:	O.K., that makes sense. But why do you live by yourselves in the forest?
HAPPY:	Hey, we like it here. We've got great neighbors. Why just in the next forest there's Little Red Riding Hood and her grandmother.
SLEEPY:	Yeah, and Sleeping Beauty has a small house just around the corner. Although, when she eventually gets kissed by that handsome prince, she'll probably want to move into his castle by the swamp.
SNOW WHITE:	Hey, you'll get no complaints from me on that one. I'd give a million dollars to have some Prince Charming come into my life just about now.
GRUMPY:	Well, maybe we could contact the Wicked Witch and arrange for something.
SNOW WHITE:	No, that's O.K. Let me get to know you a little better before we change the plot of this tale. So, anyway, tell me about this diamond mine of yours.
BASHFUL:	Well, that, too, is in the forest. We go there every day singing our song and working from dawn to dusk. We're able to mine lots of diamonds, but for some reason we don't get rich. We still live in a cramped cabin in the woods, dress in outdated clothes, and never cash in on our success.
SNOW WHITE:	Have you ever thought about talking with your writers so you could get a better setting for the story?

DOPEY:	No, we just sort of stay in this setting. I guess it was just easier for the folks over at the Disney studios to illustrate us if we stayed right here.
SNOW WHITE:	But aren't you scared living here by yourselves?
DOC:	Not really. Oh sure, we heard about that incident with the Goldilocks woman and the breaking-and-entering incident at the Three Bears' house. But we just thought that was a one-time thing.
SNOW WHITE:	(*sweeping her hands*) Well, then, tell me why your cabin is in such a mess. Clothes all over the place, it's covered with dust, and there's piles of dirty dishes in the sink.
SNEEZY:	(*a-CHEW*) Well, we were just hoping that some really nice story character (*a-CHEW*) would come over and clean up after us (*a-CHEW*).
SNOW WHITE:	(*staring angrily*) I hope you weren't thinking about me.
BASHFUL:	No, no, no. We meant some character who's had experience in scrubbing floors—like Cinderella, for example.
SNOW WHITE:	Good, because I wouldn't want to break any of my fingernails or ruin my complexion with meaningless housework.
GRUMPY:	Hey, wait a minute. I'm having a problem here. In the first place, why are we having this conversation? I mean, why do you need to have US in YOUR story?
SNOW WHITE:	Hmmmmmmm. You know, I'm not sure. I DO KNOW that this is a story about ME. It's a story about how my evil stepmother gives me a poisoned apple which I eat and then fall asleep. And then a really handsome dude on his white horse comes along and plays a little kissy-face with me. Then, I wake up and we ride off into the sunset to live happily ever after. You know, the more I think about it, the more I'm convinced you guys are completely unnecessary.

DOPEY: Yeah, we've never been able to figure that out either. After all, the real story is about you and that handsome prince fellow. We're sort of just a bunch of extras.

HAPPY: You know, you're absolutely right. I think we'd better end this conversation right now so that Snow White can get back to her main story line and we can get back to our diamond mine. To be perfectly honest—no offense, of course—you don't need us and we don't need you.

SNOW WHITE: Wow, what insight. Gosh, now I can have my own story, you guys can have your own story, and maybe all of us can live happily ever after.

NARRATOR: Aren't you forgetting something?

SNOW WHITE: Yeah! Now all I have to do is find some hunka hunka prince to star with me in another story. Is there anybody out there (*points to audience*) who wants to be my Prince Charming?

The Underappreciated Fairy Godmother (Known As Roxanne to Her Friends) Gets Really Ticked Off

STAGING: For this presentation the narrator should be placed at a podium or lectern near the center of the staging area. Note that the audience has several parts throughout the production.

Really Beautiful Cinderella Lady
X

Really Handsome Prince Guy
X

Roxanne, The Underappreciated Fairy Godmother
X

Narrator
X

Audience
X X X X X X X
X X X X X X X X

NARRATOR: You all remember the story about Cinderella? You know, the girl who spent her days scrubbing kitchen floors down at the local castle until the fairy godmother comes along and magically turns her into some really beautiful damsel and then magically turns a pumpkin into some luxury coach and magically turns the mice into her personal servants. And then, Cindy goes off to the ball where she meets a real hunk of a prince, loses her shoe, he finds her, has her try on the shoe, they marry, and yadda, yadda, yadda. You remember all that?

AUDIENCE: (*somewhat indignantly*) Yes, oh great and magnificent Narrator, we remember.

NARRATOR: O.K., let's not get testy here. Anyway, as I was saying, everybody in that story lives happily ever after except for one individual.

AUDIENCE: And who might that be, oh great and magnificent Narrator?

NARRATOR: Well, you see, everybody got so wrapped up in all that "happily ever after" stuff that nobody paid attention to what happened to the Fairy Godmother.

ROXANNE, THE UNDER-APPRECIATED FAIRY GODMOTHER: That's right, oh great and magnificent Narrator. You see, most people were so into Cindy and that really handsome dude, I mean prince, that they sort of forgot about me. But, let's face it, if it hadn't been for me the whole story wouldn't have happened at all.

REALLY HANDSOME PRINCE GUY: What do you mean, oh most lovely Fairy Godmother?

ROXANNE, THE UNDER-APPRECIATED FAIRY GODMOTHER: (*angrily*) Well, just look—and I'm tellin' you, the more I think about it the more I'm really getting ticked off about the whole thing—I'm the one who provided Cindy with that stunning low-cut evening gown with all the lace and frills and stuff. Do you think it was easy putting that thing together? No way, José. And then, our heroine just waltzes off to her fancy palace ball without so much as one word of thanks. NOT ONE WORD OF THANKS!

NARRATOR: Wow, you must have been really ticked off!

AUDIENCE: That's right, oh great and magnificent Narrator!

ROXANNE, THE UNDER-APPRECIATED FAIRY GODMOTHER: (*emphatically*) And that's not all! After Cindy gets all dolled up in her drop-dead gorgeous dress, I have to go out and find some pumpkin—a PUMPKIN, mind you—to wave my magic wand over and transform into a royal coach that takes her to the palace. (*to audience*) Now, I don't know how much you know about magic wands, but turning a pumpkin into some flashy street rod isn't the easiest thing in the world. It really took a lot of creativity to make THAT happen. Now, don't get me wrong—I was happy to do it for the sake of the story, but did I get any thanks for it? No one, not one single solitary person ever came around and thanked me for creating that beautiful coach . . . not Cindy, not anyone else in the story, not even the writer.

REALLY BEAUTIFUL CINDERELLA LADY: Gosh, I didn't know it meant all that much to you. I was in such a hurry to get off to the ball that I really didn't think about it. And, besides, the writer didn't give me any lines about thanking you.

ROXANNE, THE UNDER-APPRECIATED FAIRY GODMOTHER: (*motherly*) Look, Cindy, you're a nice kid and all that. And I hope you're very happy living with the Handsome Prince Guy at the palace. But one of these days, you're just going to have to think about other people—or fairy godmothers, as the case may be—and give them some appreciation once in a while.

NARRATOR: Gosh, it sounds like you're getting totally irritated now.

AUDIENCE: (*sarcastically*) How perceptive, oh great and magnificent Narrator.

ROXANNE, THE UNDER-APPRECIATED FAIRY GODMOTHER: Let's be honest here. If it weren't for me the story would've never happened. Cindy wouldn't have met the Really Handsome Prince Guy and they never would've lived happily ever after in the big fancy castle on the hill. But do I get any thanks? NOOOOOOOOOO! All I get is a couple of lines and a chance to show off my magic powers, but nobody—and I mean NOBODY—ever thanked me. And I'm tellin' you, I'm really ticked!

NARRATOR: Well, what can we do to change that?

AUDIENCE: Hey, oh great and magnificent Narrator, WE KNOW what to do.

(At this point, all the members of the audience come up on stage and parade past Roxanne, The Fairy Godmother, and shake her hand and say "thank you for a great story" to her. They all return to their seats.)

ROXANNE, THE UNDER-APPRECIATED FAIRY GODMOTHER: Gosh, that was really nice of all of you. And in appreciation, I'd like to do something for all of you *(waves her magic wand over the audience)*. And now, you have all been magically transformed into... REALLY HANDSOME DUDES and INCREDIBLY BEAUTIFUL DUDETTES!

NARRATOR: And you all lived happily ever after!

Teachers Live in the School Basement and Never Come Out at Night

STAGING: The narrator can be seated on a tall stool or be placed behind a lectern or podium. The other characters should be standing and interacting with one another.

```
                              Billy
                               X

                 Bianca                   Bobby
                   X                        X

                 Bonnie                   Bubba
                   X                        X

                           Barbara
                              X

Narrator
   X
```

NARRATOR:	Once upon a time, it was the beginning of a new school year. Let's listen in to the first-grade students.
BILLY:	This is the first day of school. And I'm scared!
BIANCA:	I wonder what our teacher will be like.
BOBBY:	I hear all the teachers are old. And bald. And wrinkly.

BONNIE: I hear all the teachers live in the school basement and never come out at night.

BUBBA: This summer my older brother told me that the teachers and the principal always live in the basement. The teachers and the principal come out in the morning. And they go back to the basement after everyone leaves school in the afternoon. The teachers and the principal sleep on piles of straw and catch rats and black widow spiders to eat for dinner. I also learned that the principal is really a very old teacher who can yell louder than all the other teachers. That's why he is the boss of the school.

BARBARA: I don't think I want to go to this school.

BILLY: A second-grade boy at the bus stop said that teachers are never allowed to go to the bathroom during the day. They have a special place down in the basement where they take care of that after all the students leave in the afternoon. That's why teachers are always so mean. And grouchy!

BIANCA: Another kid told me that teachers put their cars in the parking lot, but they're not allowed to drive them. Teachers' cars must be old. And rusty. And have lots of scratches.

BOBBY: A girl told me that teachers have to stay dressed up and wear the same clothes every day. They can't wear stuff like T-shirts and shorts. She said if they do they're arrested and put in jail in Kansas or France. Where they eat giant rats. And giant spiders.

BONNIE: I'm not sure I want to meet our teacher.

BUBBA: When we were riding the bus to school, a third-grade kid said that teachers get older faster than anyone else. That's because of a special ingredient in their red pens that makes their skin wrinkle and their hair and teeth fall out. He said it's against the law for teachers to use anything else but red pens to mark students' papers.

BARBARA: Someone in the back of my bus said that teachers always put fake pictures of babies and other people on their desks. That's to make everyone think they have children when they really don't. And another kid said that teachers are sent away to Arizona if they ever have children of their own. He told us that his teacher was going to have a baby, but after a couple of months no one ever saw her again. He said that teachers in Arizona make kids eat cactus for lunch. And wrestle gila monsters in gym class.

BILLY: I don't think I want to go to any school this year.

BIANCA: When we were waiting in the school lobby, an older girl said that teachers aren't allowed in any movie theaters or restaurants. That's because they always try to put everyone in straight lines or in alphabetical order. Also, teachers always tell people to "be quiet and stand up straight" whenever they're in a supermarket or department store. That's why they have to stay in the school basement.

BOBBY: The boy standing in front of me said that substitute teachers are meaner than regular teachers. That's because they have to eat all the leftover spinach in the school cafeteria. Subs also have to wash all the blackboards in the school and practice saying things like, "Karen, what is the state capital of Pennsylvania?" to the principal every day. He said that when substitutes become real teachers they have to move into the school basement with all the other teachers. And start eating rats. And spiders.

BONNIE: I don't think I'm going to like being in this school.

BUBBA: When we were walking down the hallway I heard people talking in the Teacher's Room. The kid beside me said that the teachers probably are planning an escape from the basement tonight. And they might take prisoners. And go to Arizona. He looked worried. So am I.

BARBARA: And so am I!

NARRATOR: When the kids went into their classroom they sat down in brand new desks. Miss Swanson, their teacher, was in the front. She welcomed them all to first grade. She was young, had pretty black hair, and smiled a lot. She told them, "This is going to be the best school year ever." She didn't look like she lived in a basement. Or ate spiders. Or was bald. I guess first-graders still have a lot to learn about teachers.

King Arthur and the Knights of the Polygon Table

STAGING: The narrator can be in the front and to the side of the characters. The characters can be on tall stools or can walk around the staging area interacting with each other.

Sir Dumb-a-lot	Sir Ask-a-lot	Sir Know-a-lot
X	X	X

Sir Lance-a-lot	Sir Handsome-a-lot	King Arthur
X	X	X

Narrator
X

NARRATOR: (*rambling*) Our story begins in a distant time in a distant land when knights were bold and young maidens were always getting themselves into trouble with the local fire-breathing dragon and had to be rescued by one of the bold knights and returned to her castle . . . well, anyway I think you've got an idea about when and where this story takes place. So, my part is done, but I'll be back later in the story. For now, I'm outta here (*leaves*).

KING ARTHUR: O.K. men, let's have a meeting.

21

SIR DUMB-A-LOT: Why?

KING ARTHUR: Well, just because.

SIR ASK-A-LOT: Just because why?

KING ARTHUR: Well, because we're a bunch of people who work together and when a bunch of people work together they're always supposed to have meetings.

SIR KNOW-A-LOT: And that's what we call "focused organizational interfacing."

EVERYBODY: HUH?

KING ARTHUR: Well, anyway, we need to have a meeting so that we can, uh, um, er figure out what we should be doing with all these dragons that keep roaming the countryside and running off with all the pretty young maidens.

SIR LANCE-A-LOT: (*boldly*) Then a meeting it shall be!

SIR ASK-A-LOT: Well, where shall we meet?

SIR DUMB-A-LOT: Why don't we meet in the dungeon? The light's not great, but it's got great sound effects.

KING ARTHUR: No, I don't think that's the right place.

SIR HANDSOME-A-LOT: Why don't we meet out on the castle patio with the golden rays of sunshine beaming down on our golden locks and finely chiseled physical features?

SIR KNOW-A-LOT: (*to Sir Handsome-a-lot*) I think you've been spending too much time looking in mirrors. You ought to get out more often.

SIR LANCE-A-LOT: Perhaps, we could meet in the ballroom. It's big, it's open, and it's got lots of room for a table.

SIR DUMB-A-LOT: A table?

SIR ASK-A-LOT: A table?

SIR HANDSOME-A-LOT: A table?

SIR KNOW-A-LOT: Yes, a table. It's a wooden structure typically supported by four legs upon which various and sundry articles can be placed or around which individuals may locate themselves in the pursuance of a pleasurable repast.

EVERYBODY: Huh?

SIR DUMB-A-LOT: But, why do we need a table for a meeting?

SIR LANCE-A-LOT: Because it is a way we can talk among ourselves and share ideas and reach meaningful conclusions.

KING ARTHUR: And because we work together, we should plan together. And, a table is an excellent piece of furniture to have in any castle—just ask the queen.

SIR ASK-A-LOT: Fine, but what shape should the table be?

SIR HANDSOME-A-LOT: Say again?

SIR ASK-A-LOT: I said, what shape should the table be?

SIR DUMB-A-LOT: Why should the shape make a difference?

SIR LANCE-A-LOT: Well, good friend, it may stimulate conversation and help us reach our goals.

KING ARTHUR: So, does anyone have any ideas?

SIR KNOW-A-LOT: Perhaps the table should be in a form in which the surface area has no lines of discontinuity and the placement of chairs thereof are all equidistant from the centermost point.

EVERYBODY: Huh?

SIR HANDSOME-A-LOT:	I think he means a circle.
SIR LANCE-A-LOT:	Well, that's one possibility. Anyone have any other ideas?
SIR DUMB-A-LOT:	How 'bout a square table?
KING ARTHUR:	No, as you'll notice, there are more than four people here so a square table would leave someone out.
SIR HANDSOME-A-LOT:	What about a rectangular table?
SIR LANCE-A-LOT:	No, I'm afraid that wouldn't work either. We'd probably have the same problem as before.
SIR ASK-A-LOT:	Hey, I know, what 'bout a giant triangular table.
KING ARTHUR:	Sorry, Ask-a-lot, I don't think that will work either.
SIR DUMB-A-LOT:	Well, one of my buddies who was taking a geometry class last year was talking a lot about parallelograms. Why not a parallelogram table?
SIR HANDSOME-A-LOT:	Sounds interesting, but won't that cause all kinds of decorating problems in the Great Hall? How would we position it? How would we decorate it? You can see that we'd have lots of problems with that kind of shape.
KING ARTHUR:	Boy, it looks like we're stuck. We still need to have a meeting, but we just can't decide on a shape for the table we need for the meeting.
SIR KNOW-A-LOT:	(*excitedly*) I've got it! A polygon table!
EVERYBODY:	Huh?
SIR KNOW-A-LOT:	No, really. Just think about it. A polygon is defined as a closed plane figure having more than four angles and sides.
EVERYBODY:	Huh?

SIR KNOW-A-LOT: It's perfect. A polygon table will allow all of us to sit around and discuss our adventures and make decisions and set some organizational goals. It will also permit us to add new members—you know, any new knights that we want to join this great and noble group. And, best of all, it will be easy to decorate and place in the Great Hall.

SIR LANCE-A-LOT: Wow! That's a super idea. Why didn't I think of that?

SIR KNOW-A-LOT: Well, you don't think the author gave me the name "Sir Know-a-lot" just because I'm pretty, do you?

NARRATOR: (*returning*) And so it was that the knights of King Arthur's court were able to decide on a shape for their famous table and they became known far and wide as "King Arthur and the Knights of the Polygon Table." Unfortunately, sometime during the Middle Ages there was a not-too-bright editor who didn't know his geometric shapes. When he was typing up the title for the book, he didn't know what a "polygon" was—in fact, the only shapes he did know were "round" and "square." So, he flipped a coin. Since it came up heads he changed the word "polygon" to "round" and ever since the story has been known as "King Arthur and the Knights of the Round Table." But, you (*points to audience*) and I know the real story and the real truth behind that famous piece of furniture.

Hansel and Gretel Are Beautiful and Smart but Have Really Weird Names

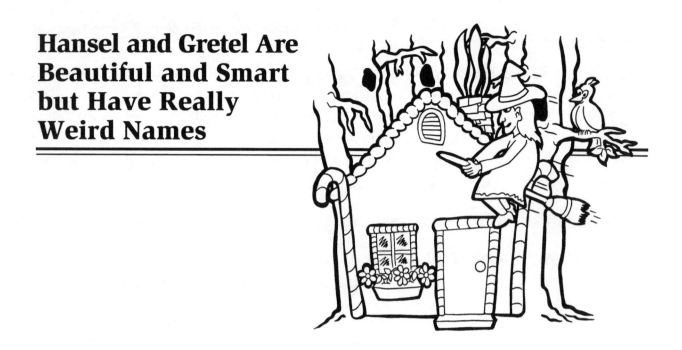

STAGING: The narrator should be seated on a tall stool to the side of the two major characters. Hansel and Gretel should be standing throughout the production. The Wicked Witch can walk onto the staging area when her parts come up (and then exit each time). Throughout the performance the Wicked Witch talks only to the audience and does not interact with the other characters.

```
              Hansel              Gretel
                X                   X

                                              Wicked Witch
                                                   X

Narrator
   X
```

NARRATOR: First of all, take a good look at our two major characters (*points*). Don't you think they are the most intelligent and best-looking characters any author could hope for in his story? For example, just look at Gretel there. Wow, is she beautiful or what? She's the most gorgeous character anyone has ever seen. And, talk about smart! Holy, moley, she's so intelligent that she makes Einstein look like a nerd. And, then look at Hansel. Wow, what a dude! Bright eyes and muscles all over the place. I mean, we're talking about a real hunk here. And not only that, but he's got some smarts that go just beyond incredible. So, take a good look at these two . . . they are one handsome and intelligent couple. Boy, if the author of this story could see these two gorgeous people, he'd probably be flippin' out just about now. Man-o-man, WHAT A PAIR!!!

HANSEL: All right, already, Narrator person. I know I'm so good looking that all the girls in town are just begging me for a date.

GRETEL: And I'm soooooooo intelligent that all the guys in town just want to be near me so that some of my smarts will rub off on them.

HANSEL AND GRETEL: YEAH, WE ARE JUST SOOOOOOOOOO FABULOUS!

WICKED WITCH: Hey, how come all the cute people get the best lines in this script?

NARRATOR: O.K., so where were we? Oh, yeah, (*mumbling*) let's see, hmmmmmmmmm, oh, yes, now I've got it. (*louder*) This is where the author has Hansel and Gretel leaving their house to go for a stroll in the deep dark forest—you know, the deep dark forest that's full of really mean and ugly wicked witches.

WICKED WITCH: There goes that Narrator again—picking on the ugly people once more. (*in a sinister voice*) But just wait, I may have something up my sleeve that not even the narrator or the writer of this story knows about.

NARRATOR: And so, once upon a time, Hansel and Gretel—the really smart and really beautiful couple—go for a walk in the forest. And because they are smart and because they don't want to get lost they leave a trail of bread crumbs from their peanut butter and jelly sandwiches along the trail so that they can find their way back at the end of the story. They don't want to be late for their next story, you know. So, anyway, there they are strolling along just minding their own business.

GRETEL: Hey, Hansel, you know we are certainly the most wonderful, most beautiful, and most intelligent couple that ever walked the face of the earth.

HANSEL: You sure have that right, oh wise and delightful one.

GRETEL: But, you know, oh pretty and clever one, I've never been able to figure out why we have these really stupid names. After all, how many other people do you know with the names "Hansel" and "Gretel?"

HANSEL: You know, you're absolutely right, oh divine and witty one. I wonder whether the writer was, as they say, "out to lunch" when he gave us these names. Surely, no sane parent in the world would ever name their children "Hansel" or "Gretel."

GRETEL: How astute, oh stunning and ingenious one. I'm beginning to think that the writer of this story really has some serious mental problems. Not only did he give us some really dorky names, but he also had the audacity to make us walk through some deep dark forest eating peanut butter and jelly sandwiches and hoping we'd bump into some weird house made out of gingerbread with a wicked old witch living inside.

WICKED WITCH: There they go again.

HANSEL: Right again, oh ravishing and bright one. You know, with our good looks and highly developed minds we should be in a story that emphasizes all our wonderful and delightful attributes. Why we're in this story, with its silly plot and not too bright narrator, is beyond me.

WICKED WITCH: Hey, what about me?

GRETEL: Well, oh attractive and resourceful one, what do you suggest we do?

HANSEL: First, we need to get rid of the narrator . . . (*to Narrator*) no offense, of course. Then we need to lose the Wicked Witch. I mean, she's O.K., I guess, because her ugliness tends to emphasize our great beauty and charm. But, she really doesn't do much for our story.

WICKED WITCH: Hey, that's O.K., I was sorta getting tired of this silly story anyway. I'd rather be eating salamander eyes, casting spells on princes, and polishing my broomstick anyway. So, I'll see ya . . . I'm outta here (*exits*).

NARRATOR: No problema! I'd rather be working in a story that better uses my finely tuned acting talents anyway. So, adios—I'm going to look for another writer and another story. Ta ta (*exits*).

GRETEL: Well, here we are, oh splendid and shrewd one. Now we have the entire story to ourselves. I guess the first thing we need to do is get some new names. We have to ditch "Hansel" and "Gretel" right away. And maybe we need to get a new writer, too. You know, one who will better emphasize our incredible good looks and fantastic intelligence.

HANSEL: And maybe we should get an agent, too. By the way, I'm hungry. Do you happen to have part of your peanut butter sandwich left?

NARRATOR: (*from offstage*) And so it was that Hansel and Gretel never really went into the deep dark forest. They did, however, get an agent and eventually changed their names to _____ and _____. (*Note: Use the names of two popular movie actors.*) And, you might ask, whatever happened to the Wicked Witch? Well, she just spent the rest of her life eating little pieces off her gingerbread house and talking with the chipmunks.

A Story About Hercules, Paul Bunyan, and the Very Tall Individual Who Lives at the Top of a Beanstalk

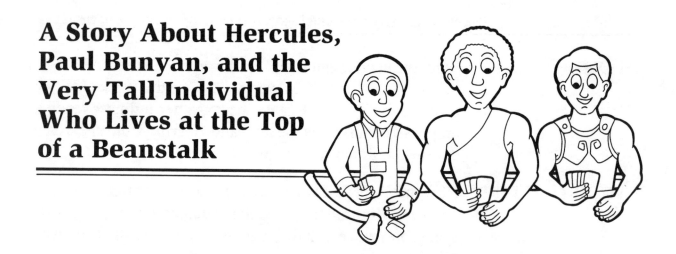

STAGING: The narrator can be placed on a tall stool to the side of the staging area. The characters can be on chairs or can be standing throughout the production.

```
                                                              Author
                                                                X

              Hercules           Paul Bunyan          Giant
                 X                    X                 X

Narrator
   X
```

NARRATOR: Well, to get things started, this is sort of a strange story. How strange, you might ask? Well, it's so strange that I'm not really sure how the author was ever able to get these three major characters together. Just think about it, first we have this character from mythology.

HERCULES: That's me, of course. And being a mythological character you'll notice how handsome I am and how wonderfully sculpted my finely tuned body is. In fact, I'm so gorgeous that all the young goddesses are madly in love with me.

NARRATOR: Well, I think I'd better step in here now before young Hercules here falls in love with himself. While you're checking this guy out, you'll probably also notice that he's extremely strong. (*Hercules breaks a thin piece of wood over his knee.*)

30

AUDIENCE:	Ohhhhhhhhhhhhhhhhhhh!
NARRATOR:	Well, let's not spend too much time with young Hercules. There's some other characters you need to meet.
PAUL BUNYAN:	Yeah, like me!
NARRATOR:	Now, here's where this story starts to get a little confusing. O.K., we have another really big and really strong story character—Mr. Bunyan here. And, as you can see, he's rippling with muscles, he's as big as a skyscraper, and he's not too bad-looking either.
PAUL BUNYAN:	And let's not forget how strong I am. Remember that time when I was walking through the desert and was so tired that I let my ax drag behind me? When I got through walking that day I turned around and there was the Grand Canyon in the ground behind me. Yeah, that was me who created that great natural wonder.
NARRATOR:	I think I should mention something at this point in our story. Not only are these guys (points to Hercules, Paul Bunyan, and the giant) big and strong, but they also have egos about as big as the planet Jupiter. Yeah, they're nice people and all that, but they do tend to love themselves a little too much—if you know what I mean.
PAUL BUNYAN:	Hey, little tiny narrator person, how would you like me to crumple you up like this? (*crumples up a sheet of paper*)
NARRATOR:	Ah, no thanks. But you will let me continue on with this story about oversized story characters, won't you?
PAUL BUNYAN:	What do you think, Hercules? Do you think we should let this tiny runt of a narrator continue with the story?
HERCULES:	Yeah, I guess it's O.K. After all, if we don't like what the narrator says we can just (*breaks a pencil in half*).
NARRATOR:	O.K., O.K., I get the message. I'll get the story moving here and introduce this fellow over here (*points to Giant*). Now,

as you've noticed, so far we have the handsome and strong Hercules from mythology, the very large and equally powerful Paul Bunyan from American folklore, and now I'd like to introduce you to the Giant person who comes to us from a French folktale in the seventeenth century. Like his friends here, he's big and tall and extremely powerful. He's also got a big mouth . . .

GIANT: (*loudly*) Hold on, just a second here, oh teeny tiny narrator person. Yeah, I've got a big mouth, but that's not my fault. You know how it is with us large people—the bigger we are, the bigger our body parts . . . and that includes our facial features such as the mouth. Yeah, I've got a big mouth, but that doesn't mean I've got a BIG MOUTH! Understand?

NARRATOR: Yeah, I get the message. So, as I was saying—now we've got three characters here—all from different kinds of stories, all from different historical times, and all from different cultures. And about now, you're probably asking yourself, why have a story with three very large individuals in it? What can they do together, that they can't do separately?

HERCULES: Well, I'm incredibly handsome, so that means all the girls will fall head over heels in love with me.

ALL GIRLS: Ohhhhhhhhhhhhhhh, Awwwwwwwwwwwww, Wowwwwwwwwww!

PAUL BUNYAN: And I'm so powerful and strong that I can create natural landmarks all over the countryside.

ALL GIRLS: Hunka, hunka, hunka, hunka, hunka, hunka!

GIANT: And I'm so tall and mighty that I can guard all the beanstalks all over the country.

ALL GIRLS: Say, what?

NARRATOR: Anyway, we have these three delightful specimens of strength and power and height and force and . . . hmmmmm, come to think about it, I'm not really sure WHY these three guys are in this story together. Hey, author person, WHY ARE these three large people in this one story?

AUTHOR: (*walking onstage*) Hey, look, I'm just trying to make a living. Somebody told me that almost every folktale or fairy tale had to have some sort of large individual or someone with a really mean temper or someone who was very pretty and would fall sleep after eating a poisoned apple and would then be awakened by the kiss from a handsome and dashing young prince and so on and so on and so on . . . Anyway, I think you get the message.

NARRATOR: No, not really.

AUTHOR: Well, oh character with the tiny brain, it's like this. After making up all those stories with the same plots—you know, princes saving damsels in distress, dragons breathing fire on everyone, tall people who always have attitude problems, and animals that talk—I just decided that it was time to shake things up a bit.

NARRATOR: What do you mean?

AUTHOR: Well, I thought it might be neat to get three very large and very recognizable story characters together—not because they're big and strong . . .

ALL CHARACTERS: Say what?

AUTHOR: Hey, just let me continue. When I looked at all the stories I found that most of them had big guys solving their problems with might and strength. But none of the stories had big guys solving their problems with their minds.

ALL CHARACTERS: Say what?

AUTHOR: That's right. Most all of the stories from "once upon a time" time involved large characters who knew how to throw their weight around. But the authors of those stories never talked about the intelligence of those characters. In other words, the big guys never got a chance to show how smart they were or to demonstrate that just because you're large doesn't mean you're not intelligent.

HERCULES: Hey, you know he's right. Just because I'm so good looking and big doesn't mean I'm not smart.

PAUL BUNYAN: Yeah, and just because I'm the largest character in American folklore doesn't mean I can't use my head, too.

GIANT: Yeah, you guys are right. Just because I'm the biggest character to live on top of a beanstalk doesn't mean I can't demonstrate my brain power too.

AUTHOR: That's exactly right, guys. So, what do you say? How about we get together and create a story where we can show the world how incredibly intelligent you are, how you can solve problems with your brains instead of your fists, and how people should be judging you, not by your size, but by your smarts?

ALL CHARACTERS: Yeah! Yeah! Yeah!

NARRATOR: And so it was that the author and the three biggest characters in storyland went off to create some new plots and new scripts. And years later, all the kids in the world read stories like "Hercules Solves a Very Difficult Math Problem," "Paul Bunyan Reads All the Books in the Public Library," and "The Giant Finds True Happiness as a Mechanical Engineer." And, of course, they all lived happily ever after.

Actually, the Toilet Overflowed and Thirty-Four Lizards Danced Through My Room

STAGING: The characters should be seated on chairs or tall stools throughout the production. The narrator can walk from character to character during the course of the production.

Narrator
X

Student 1
X

Student 2
X

Student 3
X

Student 4
X

Student 5
X

Student 6
X

NARRATOR: Hey, guys, what's up? How come everyone looks so sad?

STUDENT 1: Well, you see, last Tuesday, when the teacher asked me for my homework I told her I didn't have it because the dog got sick and threw up all over it. After that my little brother stuffed it in his dirty diaper and then tore it into tiny little pieces and ate them which made him sick and we had to take him to the hospital where we waited and waited and waited for him to get X-rays and a shot (in his you-know-where). And on the way back the car got three flat tires and ran out of gas twice and it wasn't until after midnight when finally we got home. And, that's why I didn't have enough time to redo the 22 math problems I was supposed to do.

NARRATOR: That's not what really happened, is it?

STUDENT 1: No, actually, the toilet overflowed and washed all my homework papers out to the street and into the sewer where they went in the ocean and were swallowed by an octopus with pimples.

NARRATOR: What happened to you?

STUDENT 2: Well, when my Dad asked me why I hadn't raked the leaves in the backyard I told him about the green-ish, purple-ish wind creature who lives in a deep-ish, square-ish hole behind the garage. Each day it sneaks out and blows leaves all over the yard every time I try to put them into piles. And sometimes the wind creature (who can also burp blue bubbles) slithers over to Jimmy's house and Eric's house and blows leaves all over *their* yards and that's why *their* fathers are mad at them, too. But, the three of us are building an electromagnetic trap (filled with slimy slugs and snails) to capture the green-ish, purple-ish wind creature so that it won't bother any other kids; because all of us *really want* to rake the leaves in our yards.

NARRATOR: That's not what really happened, is it?

STUDENT 2: No, actually, all the squirrels come out every night and cover the ground with exactly four layers of leaves so they can walk across the lawn without getting their feet dirty.

NARRATOR: Oh, I see. Well, then, what happened to you?

STUDENT 3:   You see, when my older sister (the one with funny ears) asked me if I knew where her favorite sweater was, I said that I was sure a miniature tribe of spidery faced aliens carried it into the basement closet. I told her that they were probably tearing it apart to get a special ingredient from the yarn which they needed to power their starship back to the Apricot Planet. Then, they would be able to save their world from destruction by an intergalactic band of gigantic flying turtles who were also planning to take over the universe by zapping all humans and turning them into squawking chicken heads.

NARRATOR: But, that's not what really happened, is it?

STUDENT 3:   No, actually, my best friend used the sweater to wash his bicycle, wipe the oil under his dad's car, and clean up some doggie piles in the backyard.

NARRATOR: O.K., and what about you?

STUDENT 4:   Well, when my mother asked me why I hadn't cleaned up my room I told her that I had. But, during the night a cross-eyed platypus (with incredibly bad breath) came in and tied me up and took everything I owned and threw all of it at me to try and make me tell him where the double dutch chocolate chip cookies were hidden in the kitchen. But, I was too cool and he never got me to tell him about my secret hiding place for cookies (they're always inside the bag of cat litter). But, when he left he took my favorite high top sneakers (the really stinky smelly skunky ones) and put footprints all over the walls and ceiling—and that's why my room is such a mess.

NARRATOR: But, that's not what really happened, is it?

STUDENT 4:   No, actually, thirty-four red-haired lizards were dancing in my room all night long and when they got tired they used my clothes as pillows 'cause they always sleep on dirty socks and shirts at their house.

NARRATOR:	Oh, I see. And what about you?
STUDENT 5:	Well, when my grandma came to visit last week and asked me to show her the watch she had given me for my birthday, I told her that I thought it was lying on the stove the other morning when Mom was making scrambled eggs. I explained that it probably melted and got mixed into the eggs everyone ate for breakfast and that's why Dad had to fly to Russia or Egypt or someplace like that to get a special medicine (that looks like fuzzy green peanut butter) which got rid of all the melted metal in our stomachs. But, there's no need to worry because we're all O.K. now (except my belly button still looks sort of silvery).
NARRATOR:	But, that's not what really happened, is it?
STUDENT 5:	No, actually, my dumb sister mailed it to the North Pole on purpose where a polar bear sat on it and squashed it and threw it into a glacier where it was frozen solid.
NARRATOR:	And I'll bet you've got a story to tell, too.
STUDENT 6:	Yeah, when my best friend asked if he could come over to my house Saturday and spend the night, I told him he couldn't because I needed more time to work on my super magical fantastic invention (made from old toasters and car parts) which would turn brussels sprouts into strawberry ice cream and spinach into chocolate pudding. Then kids all over the world would have this nifty machine and wouldn't have to eat any more yucky vegetables that their mothers try and make them eat. Because mothers always say that eating vegetables will help you grow up big and strong and put hair on your chest and make your eyebrows bushy and curly and turn you into some kind of famous scientist and other crazy stuff like that.
NARRATOR:	But, that's not what really happened, is it?
STUDENT 6:	No, actually, I had to do my homework and clean my room.
NARRATOR:	What a bummer!

Several Twisted Tongue Twisters by Six Twisted Twister Tellers

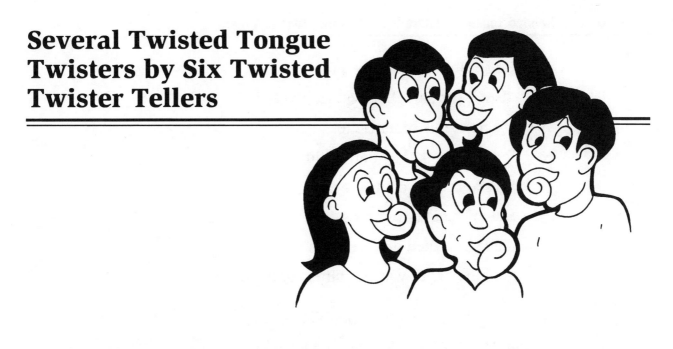

STAGING: There is no narrator for this script, nor do any of the characters have a name. (They are simply designated by numbers.) The characters can sit on chairs or on stools in a semicircle facing the audience.

```
            #3              #4
             X               X
      #2                            #5
       X                             X
   #1                                    #6
    X                                     X
```

1: Peter Piper picked a peck of pickled peppers.

Did Peter Piper pick a peck of pickled peppers?

If Peter Piper picked a peck of pickled peppers,

Where's the peck of pickled peppers Peter Piper picked?

2: How much wood would a woodchuck chuck

If a woodchuck could chuck wood?

He would chuck, he would, as much as he could,

And chuck as much wood as a woodchuck would

If a woodchuck could chuck wood.

3:   Betty Botter had some butter,

"But," she said, "this butter's bitter.

If I bake this bitter butter,

It would make my batter bitter."

So she bought a bit of butter,

Better than her bitter butter,

And she baked it in her batter,

And the batter was not bitter, only better.

4:   A big black bug bit a big black bear,

And the big black bear bled blood.

But when the big black bear bit a big bad bird,

The big bad bird bled red.

5:   She sells sea shells down by the sea shore.

The sea shore shells are shells she sells.

And the shells she sells are sea shore shells,

And sea shore shells she sells as well.

6:   A bitter biting bittern

Bit a better brother bittern,

And the bitter better bittern

Bit the bitter biter back.

And the bitter bittern, bitten

By the better bitten bittern,

Bit the biter bittern back.

[*NOTE: The following tongue twisters are shorter and should be done at a faster pace.*]

1: Rubber baby buggy bumpers. Rubber baby buggy bumpers. Rubber baby buggy bumpers.

2: Which witch wished which wicked wish? Which witch wished which wicked wish? Which witch wished which wicked wish?

3: She sifted thistles through her thistle-sifter. She sifted thistles through her thistle-sifter. She sifted thistles through her thistle-sifter.

4: Freshly-fried flying fish. Freshly-fried flying fish. Freshly-fried flying fish.

5: Fred fed Ted bread, and Ted fed Fred bread. Fred fed Ted bread, and Ted fed Fred bread. Fred fed Ted bread, and Ted fed Fred bread.

6: Six thick thistle sticks. Six thick thistles stick. Six thick thistle sticks. Six thick thistles stick. Six thick thistle sticks. Six thick thistles stick.

[*NOTE: Individuals should be paired up and perform the following tongue twisters at a rapid pace.*]

1 and 2: Toy boat. Toy boat. Toy boat.

3 and 4: Cheap ship trip. Cheap ship trip. Cheap ship trip.

5 and 6: Freshly fried fish. Freshly fried fish. Freshly fried fish.

[*NOTE: Place individuals into two teams; they should perform the following tongue twisters at a very rapid pace.*]

1, 2, and 3: Give me the gift of a grip top sock: a drip-drape, ship-shape, tip-top sock. Give me the gift of a grip top sock: a drip-drape, ship-shape, tip-top sock. Give me the gift of a grip top sock: a drip-drape, ship-shape, tip-top sock.

4, 5, and 6: The boot black bought the black boot back. The boot black bought the black boot back. The boot black bought the black boot back.

[*NOTE: Everyone performs the following tongue twister together at an extremely fast pace.*]

ALL: Ned Nott was shot and Sam Shott was not.

So it is better to be Shott than Nott.

Some say Nott was not shot.

But Shott says he shot Nott.

Either the shot Shott shot at Nott was not shot,

Or Nott was shot.

If the shot Shott shot shot Shott,

Then Shott was shot, not Nott.

But, the shot Shott shot shot not Shott, but Nott.

[*If desired, invite students to repeat all parts again.*]

Beauty and This Incredibly Ugly Guy

STAGING: Narrator I can stand to the left of the staging area; Narrator II can stand to the right. The two characters can be seated on high stools or chairs in the center. They may wish to use plastic toy phones as props.

	Ugly Guy	Beauty	
	X	X	
Narrator I			Narrator II
X			X

NARRATOR I: (*rambling and rapidly*) Once upon a time there was this deep dark forest in which there was a little cottage where this man and this woman lived with all their children and all the animals of the forest would be their friends and they ate berries and leaves and everyone was happy and smiling and just wanted to be left alone so they could eventually live happily ever after except for the fact that these out-of-work storytellers came wandering through the forest one day and decided to turn the family's life into some incredibly neat fairy tale or fable or legend or something like that so that they would all become incredibly rich and be able to live happily ever after for the rest of their lives, but do you think they even thought of sharing all their riches with that family deep in the enchanted forest? . . . No, of course they didn't; but that's probably another story which I don't have time to tell you because I'm trying to tell you this story that really isn't a real story but just a story I made up because I wanted to get rich and famous like all those other storytellers, so what I did was take one of their stories—actually I just borrowed it for a while—and decided to change just a couple of the facts and events, well, maybe I changed a lot of the facts and events, so that I could tell it to you all and you all would become incredibly excited and want to hear it again and again and want to tell your friends about this story and they would want to hear it again and again and, of course . . .

NARRATOR II: (*indignantly*) Hey, blabbermouth, just tell your stupid story.

NARRATOR I: (*to Narrator II*) Hold on to your pants! (*to the audience*) Anyway, as I was saying, before I was so rudely interrupted. Once upon a time there was this really gorgeous looking blond maiden; I mean a real knockout, a real beauty, with a fantastic personality and everything. As you might expect, all the princes from the local castle wanted to date her and take her to the movies, and concerts, and all the other kinds of things guys do with incredibly beautiful maidens. But, this incredibly ravishing young maiden didn't like all the young men in the castle—most of whom were about as stupid as a doormat anyway. Well, it just so happened that there was this really ugly guy over in the next castle. I mean, you talk about ugly . . . he was so bad he made paint peel just by being in a room. He was so ugly he had to put a bag over his head just to sneak up on a glass of water to take a drink. He was so ugly that dogs would howl whenever he walked by. He was so ugly . . .

NARRATOR II: (*loudly*) Will you just get on with the story, already?

NARRATOR I: O.K., O.K. So anyway, this really really really ugly guy wants to take the fantastically stunning young maiden out for a date. So he calls her up one evening.

UGLY GUY:	Good evening, may I please speak to the phenomenally stunning young maiden, please? (*pause*) Thank you.
	Hello, wonderfully gorgeous young maiden. This is the incredibly ugly guy.
BEAUTY:	Oh, hello. Don't you sit behind me in math class?
UGLY GUY:	Yeah, that's me. I thought you never noticed me.
BEAUTY:	Well, actually, I haven't. It's just that all the other girls have been talkin' about you. So what do you want?
UGLY GUY:	(*shyly*) Wel-l-l-l-l-l-l-l-l. You see. The Fall Ball is coming up in a few weeks down at the castle. And I was just sorta, kinda, well you see I was just thinking and wondering and maybe even kinda hopin' that . . . well, would you like to go with me to the ball?
BEAUTY:	Are you asking me for a date?
UGLY GUY:	(*unsure and rambling*) Well, yes I am. Would you like to go with me? I mean I realize that I'm certainly one of the ugliest and strangest and most repulsive creatures you've ever seen. And I'm probably not a very good dancer or anything like that. And I can barely carry on a conversation with anyone. And sometimes I have bad breath and really gross people out when I talk with them. And I'm sorta clumsy and will probably spill punch and cookies all over you. And I never take a bath and probably smell like I've been living in a sewer all my life. And I never comb my hair or brush my teeth. And my clothes are all dirty and torn and beat up and ragged and stained and all that stuff. And I never clip my toenails or wash my socks. But in spite of all that, I've got a really great personality.
BEAUTY:	Well, you know, I am sort of intrigued. I've never really gone out with an extraordinarily grotesque and hideous guy before. It sounds like it might be fun. O.K. yeah, sure, why not? Let's go out.

UGLY GUY: (*excitedly*) Oh, wow! That's great. Look, why don't I pick you up in my hay wagon next Friday night at about 7:00. O.K.?

BEAUTY: That sounds good. I'll see you then.

NARRATOR II: And so it was that this remarkably repulsive and unattractive guy was able to take the most incredibly ravishing and stunning maiden in the whole kingdom to the annual Fall Ball. And, of course, they had a great time . . . except for that time the really monstrous and unsightly guy tried to kiss the wonderfully and exquisitely beautiful young maiden. But that's another story.

Pecos Bill (A Really True Story Told by Four Honest Texans)

STAGING: In this production the four narrators tell most of the story. The narrators should all be seated on tall stools facing the audience. If desired, students may elect to have Pecos Bill "perform" his actions as the story unfolds.

	Pecos Bill	Cowboy	
	X	X	
Narrator 1	Narrator 2	Narrator 3	Narrator 4
X	X	X	X

NARRATOR I: Most people think cowboys are pretty ordinary. Well, if that's what you think, you'd be wrong. Because if there is one thing cowboys aren't—it's ordinary. Particularly if that cowboy just happens to be Pecos Bill. In fact, Pecos Bill was about as "un-ordinary" as you could possibly get.

NARRATOR II: Now, as we hear it, Bill was born back East somewhere, the youngest of 16 children. Being the smallest of all the kids, Bill always got the hand-me-downs of his brothers and sisters and never got any clothes or toys of his own. This upset Bill so much that he decided to get a toy of his own.

Like many kids, Bill wanted a teddy bear, but his parents could never afford one. So, one day he crawled out of his crib and into the woods. He waited behind a tree and before too long a mama grizzly bear walked by. Now, you know that mama bears are some of the meanest, angriest, and most bad-tempered creatures in the whole world. Only Bill didn't know that, 'cause he was only two years old and no one had told him those things before. And, because he was so young, he hadn't learned how to be scared either. Well, Bill just sprung up from behind that tree, grabbed the mama bear in a headlock, and wrestled her to the ground. The bear was so frightened that it up and died of shock right then and there. Bill picked up the bear, threw it over his shoulders, and carried it back home.

NARRATOR III: Tired from his hunt, Bill put the grizzly in his crib and fell asleep. You can imagine how surprised his parents were when they discovered Bill and his new toy. They didn't want the grizzly to go to waste so they cooked up the meat for a stew and turned the bear's coat into a blanket for Bill.

NARRATOR IV: Soon after, Bill's parents got to talking about all the new and open land that was in the West. The East was becoming too crowded, they agreed, with people living on both sides of the mountains. With 16 children, Bill's parents felt that a state as large as Texas might just be big enough to settle in and raise a family along with a couple of dogs and a dozen cats and a herd of chickens.

So Bill's parents packed all the kids, the dogs, the cats, the furniture, the pots and pans (and, of course, the chickens) into a big covered wagon and headed in the direction of the sunset. Things were going just fine until the wagon got to the Texas state line. The wagon hit the border so hard that three dogs, two cats, one chicken, and Bill bounced right out the back of the wagon. There was only one problem—because there were so many dogs, cats, chickens, and children in the wagon, nobody noticed that Bill was gone until a week later when the family arrived in the Texas panhandle. Of course, it was too late to go back and find Bill, but the family decided that anyone who could wrestle a grizzly bear could probably take care of himself no matter where he wound up.

NARRATOR I: Now you might expect that Bill, at his young age, would be scared to be all alone in the middle of nowhere. But not Bill! In fact, he felt right at home. Soon afterwards, he crawled into a nearby cave and fell fast asleep. When he woke up, he found himself in the middle of a pack of coyotes circling him and sniffing him from one end to the other. It wasn't too long before Bill and the coyotes began talking back and forth and Bill finally decided that living with a bunch of coyotes would be better than living out in the desert all by himself.

NARRATOR II: So Bill taught himself how to run like a coyote, how to hunt like a coyote, and, of course, how to howl at the moon like a coyote. In fact, before too long Bill began believing that he was a coyote. Hardly a night went by that Bill and his new "family" wouldn't sit out on the mesas and sing to the moon for most of the night. Now you may think a human and 14 coyotes howling together would be an unusual sight, but the coyotes didn't mind one bit. And, because most of the people in that part of Texas were settlers from the East, they didn't know the difference between a coyote and a baby boy.

NARRATOR III: By now you're probably wondering how Bill got the rest of his name. Well, Bill and his "family" used to roam across a part of West Texas that was cut by the Pecos River. Cowboys used to see Bill and his coyote brothers and sisters lapping up the water from the river. Pretty soon they just added the river's name to Bill's name and that's how he got to be called "Pecos Bill."

NARRATOR IV: Time went by and Bill soon found that he was quite a bit bigger than the other members of his "family." He was also starting to talk in English and began to stand upright on his two legs. Also, he noticed that he wasn't covered with fleas like the other members of the clan. He figured that he was probably some kind of strange coyote or another type of desert animal. He thought he'd better find out for sure.

So, one day, Bill wandered over to a nearby ranch and began talking with some of the cowboys there.

PECOS BILL: Howdy. I'm a coyote and I'm looking for some work.

NARRATOR I: Well, all the cowboys just laughed and laughed. They all figured that this critter was about as strange an animal as one could find.

COWBOY: Hey, you're no coyote. Just look at yourself—you walk on two legs and you don't have any tail.

NARRATOR II: Bill turned around and around and eventually discovered that something seemed to be missing. Now, this was the first time Bill noticed that he had no tail and, being a pretty smart critter, he began to suspect that he might be something other than a coyote. He also discovered that he wasn't wearing any clothes like the cowboys were. So the cowboys loaned him some clothes, washed him up, got him a cowboy hat, and invited him to work with them on the ranch.

NARRATOR III: Most cowboys today have a lariat they use to help rope cattle. But, in those days nobody had invented the lasso yet—that is, until Pecos Bill came along. It happened when Bill was out looking for lost cattle. As he rounded a mountain, a 15-foot rattlesnake sprang at him from behind a giant cactus. Bill grabbed the tail end of the rattler and swung it around and around his head so hard that it stretched out for about 30 feet or so. Eventually, all the poison and all the fight were swung out of that darned rattler. Bill just threw it over his shoulder and used it as a lariat from that day forward. Whenever a cow wandered off or got loose from the rest of the herd, Bill just took his "rope," made a lasso in one end, swung it around his head, and roped the stray cow. In fact, people agree that Pecos Bill was the first man to invent cattle roping and it's still done the same way today (except most cowboys use real rope instead of rattlesnakes).

NARRATOR IV: Bill also invented something else that Texas is known for. You see, in those days there were lots of tornadoes that twisted and tore their way across the prairies. These tornadoes were big—often as big as the whole state of Texas. They were so large and so powerful that they would just up and destroy smaller states that got in their way. (In fact, some of those states are still missing today.) Well, Bill decided that he'd had enough of those storms and one day just waited for one to come by. It wasn't too long before a big twister swung through West Texas. In no time, Bill just jumped right on the back of that twister and rode it for all he was worth. Bill and the twister flew across the land tearing up mountains and hills all over the state. (That's why most of Texas is so flat today.) For days, the twister tried to buck and kick Bill off its back, but Bill just held on for all he was worth. Eventually, he rode that twister until it was so tired it just wore itself out and turned into a gentle breeze.

NARRATOR I: Cowboys who watched the whole thing said it was the most incredible sight they had ever seen. They all wanted to try it; but of course Bill was the only one who could ride the wind. So the cowboys got some mean and angry steers and began riding them just like Bill had ridden the tornado. It wasn't too long before rodeos were invented—where bulls were roped, steers were ridden, and horses were raced. While there are lots of ornery bulls that cowboys ride in rodeos, nobody has ever ridden a tornado like Bill. In fact, you really don't see many tornadoes in that part of Texas today. Most of them have moved north to Oklahoma and Kansas and Nebraska—probably afraid of being ridden and tamed by Pecos Bill.

NARRATOR II: Bill almost met his match, though, with a horse called the Widow-maker. Now this horse was the wildest, meanest, and orneriest horse anyone had ever seen. Nobody had ever been able to tame it and it was impossible to control. Cowboys from near and far had tried to ride this creature and every one of them wound up with a broken arm or a twisted leg. Some said the horse was just plum crazy. But the horse had never met Bill before.

Bill caught up with the horse high in the mountains one day. He roped him with his rattlesnake lasso and jumped on the Widow-maker's back. Well, that horse started bucking across the better part of five states and three counties. Hour after hour and day after day the two of them tangled across the countryside. During the fifth day, Bill almost fell off the horse's back and reached out and grabbed hold of the state border between Texas and New Mexico. About that time the horse took off, heading north and running like the wind. Well, the horse was so strong that she and Bill just stretched out that borderline until it was as straight as an arrow. If you look at a map, you'll see how straight the border is between those two states—all due to Pecos Bill and the Widow-maker.

NARRATOR III: About that same time Bill was courting a young lady by the name of Slue-foot Sue. Now Sue was a character herself. In fact, the first time Bill saw Sue she was riding a giant catfish down the Pecos River. Some people say that it wasn't actually a catfish, but rather a whale she was riding. We really don't know, because whales and Texas catfish are about the same size, so it's difficult to tell them apart.

Anyway, Bill and Sue wanted to get married in a big ceremony attended by all the cowboys from across Texas. Bill wore his finest duds and Sue wore a store-bought wedding dress with a large bustle. Soon after the wedding, Sue jumped on the back of Widow-maker ready to head off for the honeymoon. Well, Widow-maker never let anyone ride her except Bill so she just turned around and bucked Sue so hard that she sent Sue sailing out and over the moon.

Sue fell back to earth and landed on her bustle—bouncing right back into outer space. Each time she fell she rocketed back up to the stars. This continued for several days until her dress caught on the "handle" of the Big Dipper. When Bill saw that, he grabbed his rope and lassoed Sue down from the skies. He brought her back to earth and the two of them lived happily ever after. But Sue never tried to ride Widow-maker again.

NARRATOR IV: Well, there you have it, ladies and gentlemen—the true and honest story about Pecos Bill. And you know it's true 'cause we're from Texas and Texans don't tell lies.

Grandmothers Are Ladies with No Children of Their Own, Funny Shoes, and Lots of Cats

STAGING: The narrators should all be seated on tall stools facing the audience.

Narrator I	Narrator II	Narrator III
X	X	X

NARRATOR I: Grandmothers are ladies with no children of their own, funny shoes, and lots of cats. Everybody should have a grandmother—they're sometimes more fun than parents, and always more fun than a baby brother.

NARRATOR II: Some grandmothers are old, but not too old that they can't take you for a chocolate chip ice-cream cone at the park or a ride on the roller coaster. Old grandmothers usually wear glasses and carry a bag full of knitting or some books so that they have something to do when you're playing on the swings.

NARRATOR III: Some grandmothers are plump—but not too plump. Plump grandmothers always get boxes of chocolates or fancy fruit in the mail, which they like to hide from their friends. A skinny grandmother is one who never bakes sugar cookies or has strawberry shortcake for her grandchildren.

NARRATOR I: It's a good idea to have a grandmother with a big lap. Then you'll have lots of room to sit down and snuggle when she tells you all those stories about the "good old days." A grandmother with a small lap means you'll always be falling off and never be able to hear the end of her stories.

NARRATOR II: Your grandmother doesn't have to be too smart—just smart enough to answer questions like, "Where do babies come from?" and "Why do girls wear underwear with pictures on them?" and "What does Grandpa do with his false teeth at night?" Some grandmothers will tell you, "That's none of your business," or "I think it's time to go to the park." That's O.K. You can always ask Grandpa those questions later.

NARRATOR III: Grandmothers should be rich, but not so rich that they move to Florida. A rich grandmother will always send you a $5.00 bill on your birthday, instead of a piece of cardboard from the bank with four quarters stuck in it.

NARRATOR I: A grandmother should have lots of change when she takes you to the shopping mall. Then you'll be able to play all the video games and toss coins into the big water fountain. A good grandmother will even let you keep the extra change.

NARRATOR II: Grandmothers always wear stockings that fall down when they walk. Never tell your grandmother about her stockings, especially when she's playing cards with her friends. If you do, she may accidentally forget about the "surprise" she was going to give you at dinner time.

NARRATOR III: Grandmothers like to talk a lot, so make sure you have one that tells you interesting things, like when your father was seven years old and fell off his bicycle into the mud, or when Grandpa lost his teeth in Atlantic City, and other neat stuff like that. A grandmother who reminds you about the time your diaper fell off is always embarrassing.

NARRATOR I: Whenever you visit, grandmothers always pinch your cheek and say things like, "My, how you've grown since we saw you last," or "You're looking more like your father every day." Be sure to smile and say something polite like, "Yes, Ma'am." You can always fix your cheek later.

NARRATOR II: Most grandmothers like to go shopping. If you visit your grandmother she'll probably take you to the mall to look at expensive silverware or lacy tablecloths. Always smile and say things like, "That's nice," or "Won't grandpa be excited." Afterwards, she'll take you to the ice cream store to get a hot fudge sundae with a double helping of whipped cream.

NARRATOR III: Your grandmother's house should have a big bed for you to sleep in when you visit. You should never have to sleep in the same room with Grandpa—especially if he snores a lot. Of course, if you snore a lot, Grandpa won't want to sleep with you, either.

NARRATOR I: Most grandmothers don't like to play tag, so make sure your grandmother has lots of games at her house. It's fun to eat brownies and play games with your grandmother on rainy day visits, but be sure to let your grandmother win every once in a while. Grandmothers like that.

NARRATOR II: Some grandmothers will make you use good manners at the table, like telling you to eat your mashed potatoes with a fork, or not to use your sleeve as a napkin, or not to feed your broccoli to the cat. Don't worry, this type of grandmother will always give you an extra slice of cherry pie at dessert time.

NARRATOR III: Grandmothers like to take lots of walks and look at things like leaves, and squirrels, and other stuff like that. A good grandmother will never tell you to hurry up. That's important, especially when you're looking for the hairiest, scariest, and ugliest caterpillar to give your sister. Grandmothers who walk fast never give you enough time to find all the bugs and snails and other crawly things you need to take back home.

NARRATOR I: Grandmothers are ladies with no children of their own. That's why they're always fun to visit. So, make sure you chose your grandmother very carefully. You don't want to be disappointed.

Goldilocks and the Three Hamsters

STAGING: The narrator sits off to the side on a tall stool or chair. The other characters can be standing or sitting in chairs.

Papa Hamster
X

Baby Hamster
X

Mama Hamster
X

Goldilocks
X

Narrator
X

NARRATOR: Once upon a time there were three hamsters. One was Baby Hamster. He was the smallest. The middle-sized hamster was Mama Hamster. The biggest hamster was Papa Hamster. They all lived together in a cage in Mrs. Johnson's classroom. One day Mama Hamster baked some hamster food in the hamster oven and put it on the hamster table for breakfast. They all stood around to eat.

BABY HAMSTER: OWWWW! This hamster food is too hot!

MAMA HAMSTER: You are right, Baby Hamster. What shall we do until it is cool?

PAPA HAMSTER: Let's go for a run on the exercise wheel on the other side of the cage. When we come back the hamster food will be just right.

NARRATOR: The hamster family left their hamster breakfast cooling on the hamster table. They walked over to the exercise wheel to go for a morning run. While they were on the wheel, a little girl named Goldilocks, who was a student in Mrs. Johnson's class, was walking by the cage. She was on her way to get her pencil sharpened. She walked by the cage and smelled the hamster food.

GOLDILOCKS: OOOHHH. That smells so good. I didn't have anything for breakfast and I'm really hungry. Maybe I'll just take a quick peek inside this cage.

NARRATOR: Goldilocks looked through the bars in the cage and into the hamster house. She opened the cage door and stuck her head right inside.

GOLDILOCKS: Look at this big bowl of hamster food. I'll have to try it. Oh, no, this is just too hot. Maybe I'll eat this middle-sized bowl. No, it is just a little too cold. I'll try this tiny bowl. Oh, yes! This is just right!

NARRATOR: Goldilocks ate all the hamster food in Baby Hamster's bowl. Then she began to look around the inside of the little hamster house. She noticed the three hollow tubes that the hamsters played in.

GOLDILOCKS: Look at those tubes. I think I'll stick my finger in the big one. Goodness! This one's too big. Maybe the middle-sized tube is better. No, it's still too big. I think this little one will be just right.

NARRATOR:	But when Goldilocks put her big fat finger inside the tiny, little tube she got stuck. She shook and shook and shook her finger until the tube flew off and smashed into a thousand pieces on the floor. That made her very angry and very upset. She decided to look around the house some more. She found the three water bottles that the hamsters used to get their drinks.
GOLDILOCKS:	Those water bottles sure do look interesting. I think I'll try them. I'll try the big one first. Oh, no, this is much too big for me. Perhaps the middle-sized one is better. No, this one's not right either. I'll try the little one. Yes, this one's just the right size. I'll use it to get a drink of water.
NARRATOR:	Goldilocks tried to pull her head out of the cage. Unfortunately, her big head got stuck in the bars. Soon, the three hamsters came back from their exercise wheel.
BABY HAMSTER:	Look, Papa! Somebody has been in our house.
MAMA HAMSTER:	Let's go in very carefully and very slowly.
PAPA HAMSTER:	SOMEONE HAS BEEN EATING MY HAMSTER FOOD!
MAMA HAMSTER:	SOMEONE HAS BEEN EATING MY HAMSTER FOOD!
BABY HAMSTER:	SOMEONE HAS BEEN EATING MY HAMSTER FOOD! And it's all gone!
NARRATOR:	The hamsters began looking around the house. Papa Hamster saw that his hollow tube had been moved.
PAPA HAMSTER:	SOMEONE HAS BEEN PLAYING WITH MY HOLLOW TUBE!
MAMA HAMSTER:	SOMEONE HAS BEEN PLAYING WITH MY HOLLOW TUBE!
BABY HAMSTER:	SOMEONE HAS BEEN PLAYING WITH MY HOLLOW TUBE! And they broke it into a thousand pieces!

NARRATOR:	The hamsters kept walking around the inside of their house. Papa Hamster was the first to see that his water bottle had been disturbed.
PAPA HAMSTER:	SOMEONE HAS BEEN MESSING WITH MY WATER BOTTLE!
MAMA HAMSTER:	SOMEONE HAS BEEN MESSING WITH MY WATER BOTTLE!
BABY HAMSTER:	SOMEONE HAS BEEN MESSING WITH MY WATER BOTTLE! And, look, there she is with her head caught in our cage.
NARRATOR:	(*faster and faster*) Goldilocks got very scared. The three hamsters began running towards her. Goldilocks pulled harder and harder. The hamsters were getting closer and closer. Goldilocks was getting more and more scared. Finally, with one last yank she pulled her head out just in the nick of time. (*slowly*) After that, she promised she would never, ever eat hamster food again. The three hamsters got a large rat to guard their house and put locks on all their doors. And they all lived happily after ever.

Merry Maid Meredith and the Kissing Lesson down at the Pond

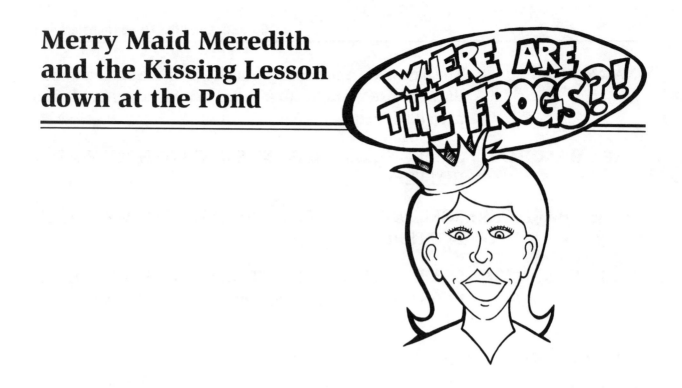

STAGING: The narrators are at a lectern or podium near the front of the staging area. The frogs are in the background and can be on chairs or tall stools. Maid Meredith and the princesses can walk around as they say their lines.

```
        Frog 1              Frog 2              Frog 3
          X                   X                   X

                                      Princess 1
                                          X
        Merry Maid Meredith                        Princess 2
               X                                       X
                                      Princess 3
                                          X

Narrator I    Narrator II
    X             X
```

NARRATOR I: (*very seriously*) The story we are about to bring you is true. The events happened just as you will see them. Only the names of the amphibians involved have been changed to protect the innocent. It happened one day at a place not too far from here, in a time not too long ago.

NARRATOR II:	Now, because you are a very bright and very intelligent audience you probably know that in "Once upon a Time" time there were a bunch of castles and these castles were always located in areas with poor drainage, today referred to as swamps. And always in the swamps there were all sorts of creatures including frogs, trolls, wicked witches, and an occasional toad or two. Well, for our purposes today, we're not going to worry about the trolls and other strange individuals because they have absolutely no part in this story. Instead, we're going to focus exclusively on the amphibious members of our friendly neighborhood pond.
NARRATOR I:	(*very seriously*) And it's all true—100% absolutely and positively true—just as you are about to see it.
NARRATOR II:	And so, because you are a very bright and very intelligent audience, you also know that in those "Once upon a Time" days the local castles were filled with beautiful princesses. And because the princesses had nothing better to do with their time than sit around and watch flies walk across the ceiling, they would frequently saunter down to the local pond and do something positively disgusting! (*pause*)
PRINCESS 1:	Look, we read in some of those other "Once upon a Time" stories that there were a bunch of really cool princes down at the pond, all cleverly disguised as frogs.
PRINCESS 2:	Yeah. And we heard from our local neighborhood sorcerer that all we had to do was to kiss the right frog and he would be turned back into a handsome dude of a prince and we could marry him and live happily ever after.
PRINCESS 3:	The only thing our friendly neighborhood sorcerer didn't tell us was how to distinguish the enchanted frogs from the non-enchanted frogs. I mean, once you've seen one frog you've seen them all. Right?
ALL FROGS:	Ribbit! Ribbit! Ribbit!

PRINCESS 1:	So, quite naturally, all we could do was to kiss each and every frog in the pond. (*The frogs all make unpleasant faces.*)
ALL FROGS:	Ribbit! Ribbit! Ribbit!
PRINCESS 2:	And I'm telling you, if you've ever tried to kiss a couple dozen frogs. . . . It's not the most sanitary thing I've ever done.
ALL FROGS:	Ribbit! Ribbit! Ribbit!
PRINCESS 3:	But that wasn't the worst of it. After we had kissed about a hundred of these precious little creatures we discovered something truly amazing—they didn't have lips. That's right, these slimy little critters (*points to frogs*) had no lips whatsoever!
PRINCESS 1:	Yeah. And have you (*points to member of the audience*) ever tried to kiss someone who doesn't have lips? It's like trying to kiss a soft-boiled egg—it's mushy and gooey and slimy and it's just plain not fun!
PRINCESS 2:	And the worst thing is they just don't do anything. They just sit there on their lily pads while we have to get down on our hands and knees, bend over into some kind of pretzel shape, and plant a big juicy one right on their mouths.
ALL FROGS:	(*very excitedly*) Ribbit! Ribbit! Ribbit!
PRINCESS 3:	We finally realized that we weren't getting anywhere. We kissed just about every lipless frog in the swamp, but nowhere could we find our enchanted princes. I mean, it was a real bummer.
NARRATOR I:	(*very seriously*) The preceding story has been absolutely true. But the next part of the story is even more absolutely true.

NARRATOR II: Now, as was the custom in "Once upon a Time" time, there was one character in the story who was more intelligent and certainly more beautiful than all the other characters put together. In this story that character is Merry Maid Meredith. Now, Merry Maid Meredith wasn't your everyday average princess. No, siree. On the one hand she was the epitome of loveliness—she was beyond pretty, she was beyond attractive, she was beyond gorgeous, she was beyond incredibly stunning, she was beyond . . .

ALL FROGS: Hubba. Hubba. Hubba.

NARRATOR I: Well, anyway, I think you get the idea. And, not only was she the most ravishing thing in the entire kingdom, she was also the brightest. In fact, she was beyond bright, she was beyond intelligent, she was beyond brilliant, she was beyond . . . well, anyway I think you get the idea. But perhaps we'd better let Merry Maid Meredith tell her side of the story.

MAID MEREDITH: Well, finally! All I've been doing for the last several minutes is stand around inside this story with nothing to do and nothing to say. Now I get my big chance.

PRINCESS 1:   So, Merry Maid Meredith, what do you think we should do about this kissing situation, or perhaps, I should say—lipless frog situation?

MAID MEREDITH: Well, I've been around, and sure I've kissed a few lipless amphibians in my time . . . and a few other lipless creatures that I won't go into now. And they're all pretty much the same.

ALL FROGS: (*very quietly*) Ribbit! Ribbit! Ribbit!

PRINCESS 2:   So, Merry Maid Meredith, what did you do? What can we do?

MAID MEREDITH: What you need to do is find that one special amphibian: the one who's different from all the others . . . the one who stands out . . . the one who's distinctive, singular, and unique.

PRINCESS 3: We've tried that, Merry Maid Meredith, but they all look the same: they're all slimy . . . they've all got webbed feet . . . they've all got big bulging eyes. . . . I mean, the reality is that once you've seen one you've seen them all.

PRINCESS 1: What you mean, Princess 3, is that once you've kissed one you've kissed them all.

MAID MEREDITH: Ahhhhhhhh. But I'm not just talking about frogs. Remember there's always more fish in the sea, or should I say there's always more amphibians in the pond.

PRINCESS 2: Hey, I'm not as bright and not as pretty as you. What exactly are you trying to say?

MAID MEREDITH: What I'm saying, girls, is this: You need to expand, you need to cast a wider net, you need to go out and beyond, you need to. . . What I'm saying is, you need to kiss something besides just frogs.

PRINCESS 3: Wow, we never thought of that. We were always told that the enchanted princes always took the shape of frogs. Wow, were we mistaken.

MAID MEREDITH: That's right, Princess 3. Don't forget that there are many different kinds of amphibians besides just frogs. Myself . . . well, I've dated a few salamanders, gone out with a couple of toads, and even held hands with a newt.

ALL PRINCESSES: (*amazed*) Ohhhhhhhhhhhhhhhh!

MAID MEREDITH: But you've got to be careful. Because if you ever do find that enchanted amphibian and he turns into a prince person, you know what happens?

ALL PRINCESSES: No we don't. Please tell us.

MAID MEREDITH: Well, after you kiss them, all they want to do is hang around and get fat and lazy and never pick up after themselves and never do the housework and always burp and watch stupid football games, and so on and so on.

ALL PRINCESSES: (*amazed*) Ohhhhhhhhhhhhh!

PRINCESS 1: So, what's your advice, Merry Maid Meredith?

MAID MEREDITH: Easy, just remember this: You can kiss them, but you don't have to take them home.

NARRATOR II: (*knowingly*) Ain't that the truth!

What Brian's Father Does

[*Author's note: This is the only "serious" script in the book. It is my hope that you and your students will discover several opportunities to talk about the power of books and the magic of reading upon the conclusion of this presentation.*]

STAGING: The narrator can be standing off to the side of the staging area. Each of the other characters can also be standing or milling about the staging area as the story is unfolding.

Angela		Carlo		Mara		
X		X		X		
	Andrew		Curtis		Ramona	
	X		X		X	
	T.J.		Brian		Jennifer	
	X		X		X	
						Narrator
						X

NARRATOR: Sunlight trickled down the walls of Miss Swanson's third-grade classroom. Angela, Carlo, Mara, Brian, and the other students were draped across desks, crushed into beanbag chairs, and tossed about the floor like rubber dolls. Everyone was quietly reading a book about famous explorers, brave heroes, and daring adventurers. When the 1:15 bell signaled afternoon recess, books were scattered into desks, shoes were retied, and an eager roar filled the room. Pouring out the door, several students raced across the baseball field to the jungle gym on the far side of the playground. Scrambling over and under the bars, they each began to boast about the brave things their fathers did.

ANGELA: (*proudly*) Hey, did you know that my father flies 747 and 757 airplanes to Los Angeles and Hawaii and even to Australia? Sometimes he packs lots of clothes and is gone for several days, but he always sends me postcards.

BRIAN: (*quietly*) That's O.K., you know. But my dad takes me on spaceship flights to Jupiter and Mars, down the rapids of dangerous South American rivers, and even through dark caverns and creepy caves deep inside the earth.

CARLO: You've got to be kidding! (*boasting*) My father works with lots of money every day. My dad gives loans to people to build bright new shopping malls and giant manufacturing plants and marinas at the shore where many boats come and go. I've even been on some of those yachts.

BRIAN: That's O.K., I guess. But did you know that my father has discovered a treasure chest on a sunken pirate ship in the Caribbean Ocean, found bags of gold in the high mountains of Peru, and located the Lost Dutchman's Mine in the Superstition Mountains of Arizona?

MARA: No way! (*bragging*) My father builds enormous office buildings all over the city. My father can stand on top of a 35-story structure, move heavy steel girders into place, and weld them together—without being scared at all. He even eats his lunch on top of the buildings he builds.

BRIAN: That's all right, I suppose. But my father has constructed castles in Germany and Spain, built adobe cave dwellings on the sides of Colorado cliffs, and assembled giant space stations that orbit the Earth. In fact, last Wednesday my dad and I made an igloo and hunted polar bears just north of the Arctic Circle.

ANDREW: Yeah, sure! (*boasting*) Listen, my father performs eight-and nine-hour operations at the hospital, has phone conferences with important doctors all across the country, and has his very own laboratory. He even has a real skeleton hanging in his office.

BRIAN: Well, I guess that's O.K. But my father has talked with medicine men in the jungles of New Guinea and Borneo, traveled to China to see how fireworks and paper were invented, and investigated an ancient Native American tribe in the deserts of New Mexico.

CURTIS: Gee, you sure have some weird stories! (*proudly*) But did you know that my dad works for an important computer company that sells computers to businesses and colleges all over the world? I have three of my father's computers at home and can e-mail people all over the world. My dad even has his own fax machine in the living room.

BRIAN: (*quietly*) I guess that's O.K. My dad and I have taken a walk inside a computer and a human body, seen the calendars and sun dials of the Mayas and Incas, and deciphered the hieroglyphics inside ancient Egyptian tombs.

RAMONA: Do you really expect us to believe all that? (*bragging*) Listen, my dad works in a fancy office building downtown. My father defends important people in court, helps clients win lots of insurance money, and often works very late at night looking at lots of legal documents. He even has two secretaries who work for him.

BRIAN: That's nice. But did you know that my dad and I have investigated bank robberies and murders in England and France, worked alongside Sherlock Holmes and the Hardy Boys, and have even helped the FBI track down several dangerous criminals across the country? Most of the cases we've worked on have been solved right in our living room.

T.J.:	No way! (*boastfully*) My father spends lots of time traveling around the country selling machine parts to big manufacturing companies, gets to stay in hotels with saunas and swimming pools and lots of tropical plants, and drives an expensive car. He does a lot of business on the cellular telephone in his car.
BRIAN:	That's O.K., I suppose. My father and I have ridden through East African jungles on the backs of lions and crocodiles, soared over Montana treetops with eagles and pterodactyls, and swum in the ocean with blue dolphins and giant squid.
JENNIFER:	Not a chance! (*proudly*) My father teaches at a very large university, does research for several major companies and organizations, and gives important speeches at conferences and conventions around the country. He even takes me to Washington, D.C., every year.
BRIAN:	That's O.K. My dad has talked to monarchs in faraway lands and distant empires, made discoveries with ancient explorers and modern day astronauts, and spoken to presidents and rulers in countries all over the globe.
ALL:	(*to Brian*) Yeah, you expect us to believe that?
BRIAN:	Well, what exactly do your fathers do?
ANGELA:	My father is a pilot for Intercontinental Airlines.
CARLO:	My father is a vice president for Metropolitan National Bank.
MARA:	My father is a foreman for Empire Construction Company.
ANDREW:	My dad is a heart surgeon at City Memorial Hospital.
CURTIS:	My dad is a manager at Consolidated Computer Company.
RAMONA:	My father is a lawyer in the firm of Johnson and Neffers.

T.J.:	My dad is a salesman for National Metal Products Company.
JENNIFER:	My father is a professor in the chemistry department at State University.
ALL:	(*to Brian*) Now, what exactly does your father do?
BRIAN:	My father reads a book to me every night!

Jack and the Tall Legume
(The Story They Never Told You)

STAGING: The narrator sits on a stool in front of the characters. The characters can be seated in chairs or standing.

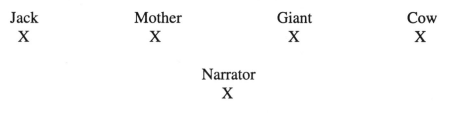

Jack	Mother	Giant	Cow
X	X	X	X

Narrator
X

NARRATOR: You all probably remember the story about Jack and his encounters with a former NBA basketball player who just happened to live at the top of a very tall bean plant. Now the writers who told you that story would have you believe that this very tall person who lived at the top of the very tall bean plant had nothing better to do with his time than eat unsuspecting little boys who just happened to climb to the top of that very tall bean plant looking for a bunch of gold to take home to their poor, starving mothers who lived around the bottom of that very tall plant. Well, it is true that giants are known far and wide for their ability to nibble, chew, and chomp on little boys. However, the version you heard of that story is not the real story—the real story is the one that you're going to hear right now.

JACK: (*excitedly*) Hey, Mom, guess what I did. I went down to the marketplace with our cow, Bessie, and sold her to this nice used car salesman for a handful of cactus seeds.

NARRATOR: (*to the audience*) You've probably guessed that Jack is not the brightest kid around. For, as everyone knows, you can't get cactus seeds from a used car salesman. But, after all, this is a fairy tale so why don't we all just pretend?

MOTHER: (*angry*) You silly boy! What do you mean you traded our best cow, in fact, our only cow, for a handful of stupid seeds from some used car salesman?

COW: (*to audience*) Yeah, think how I feel. I've just spent the last 10 years of my life giving this family some of the best milk ever produced in six counties, and this dumb kid just hauls me off to the marketplace, gets taken in by some smooth-talking salesman, and trades me for a bunch of cactus seeds. Talk about feeling bad!

MOTHER: (*still angry*) Jack, you take these stupid cactus seeds, go back down to the stupid marketplace, find that stupid sales-man, and get our stupid cow back.

COW: (*to the audience*) See what I mean. I still can't get any re-spect around here.

JACK: (*lightly*) O.K. Mom, I'll do it first thing tomorrow. In the meantime why don't you just throw these seeds out the window and let's see what happens.

NARRATOR: I'm sorry, folks, but we're going to have to stop the story right here. In the first place, because these folks live in the mountains there's no way those cactus seeds are going to sprout. As you know, cacti (that's the plural of cactus) only grow in hot, dry areas like deserts. In the second place, imagine what would happen if that cactus actually did grow 1,000 feet tall. I mean, don't you think Jack would have a really tough time trying to climb to the top of that enormous plant? Talk about getting stuck in a story! It looks like your friendly neighborhood narrator is going to have to save the day once again and change some of the dialogue so that we can continue on. So, here goes.

JACK: (*amazed*) Oh, how amazing. Those useless cactus seeds have now magically turned into some stupid bean seeds. Gosh, isn't that narrator amazing?

MOTHER: Yes, and now I can throw those stupid bean seeds out the window and we can continue on with this story.

NARRATOR: Mother throws the bean seeds out the window, a beanstalk about 5,000 feet tall grows during the night, and now it's the next morning.

JACK: (*excited*) WOW! UNBELIEVABLE! INCREDIBLE! OUT OF SIGHT!

MOTHER: What are you mumbling about now, my dear son (*looks out the window*)? Hey, holy moley, will you take a look at that enormous beanstalk! That must be the biggest thing since Billy Bob grew that incredible sunflower in the manure pile outside his barn last summer.

JACK: (*eagerly*) Well, Mother, time is wasting. This is a short story, so I better get moving and climb up this beanstalk to see what's at the top. I sure hope I don't run into any giant problems while I'm there! Get it? Giant problems.

NARRATOR: Jack begins to climb up the beanstalk. After several days, he arrives at the top only to be greeted by an enormous person with bad breath and an attitude problem—what you and I would refer to as a giant.

GIANT: (*angry*) Hey, what makes you think you can just climb up some convenient beanstalk and come into my yard? I should have you arrested and hauled off to jail.

JACK: Hey, look, Mr. Giant, I'm just following directions. The writer of this story said that I should climb up this beanstalk, sneak into your castle, run away with your golden harp and your hen that lays those incredibly golden eggs, and then live happily ever after with my mother.

GIANT: (*very angry*) Say, who is that writer anyway? Just wait until I get my hands on him!

JACK: So, do you mind if we continue on with this story?

GIANT: (*extremely angry*) Mind! You bet your little pinhead I mind. In fact, I'm getting sick and tired of all you little creeps climbing up all these beanstalks to bother me and my wife. Just look at this place. There's potato chip bags, candy wrappers, and little pieces of bubble gum left all over the yard. It's one thing to come visiting without being invited, and quite another to be complete slobs and leave all your garbage around here. The least you could do would be to clean up after yourselves. This place is beginning to look like a dump.

JACK: (*meekly*) Hey, look, this is just my first visit—actually, it's my first story with you. I'm not like all those other guys in all those other fairy tales. Honest.

GIANT: Oh yeah? Well, if that's the case then why don't you just pick up all this trash, mow my lawn, wash my windows, sweep the driveway, and paint the picket fence.

JACK: Oh, I think I hear my mother calling me for dinner. You'll excuse me.

GIANT: (*laughing*) Ha, ha, ha. That works every time.

NARRATOR: And so it was that Jack never got to steal the golden harp or run off with the hen that laid the golden eggs; those events were added by another writer. Some time later, Jack and his mother moved to Arizona and started a mail order cactus business. The giant, we hear, eventually sold his castle to some real estate developers and he and his wife moved into a condo on top of another tall vegetable. And the cow, well nobody knows what happened to the cow.

COW: (*dejectedly*) It figures!

William Tell and the Story with the Babbling Narrator

STAGING: The narrator can be walking around the staging area in a haphazard fashion as though he or she is not quite sure where to be. The writer should have an exasperated or frustrated look on his or her face throughout the production. The other characters can be seated on stools or chairs.

```
                                              Writer
                                                X

        William Tell                    Evil Ruler
             X                                X

                      Narrator
                         X
```

NARRATOR: (*singsongy*) In days of old, when knights were bold, tra la la la la la. In days of old, when knights were bold, tra la la la la la . . .

WILLIAM TELL: Hey, narrator person, any time you're ready . . . !

NARRATOR: Oh, sorry about that. I guess I was just getting carried away with the theme song to this production. (*rambling*) You know, all the other productions don't have theme songs, so I thought, well heck, why don't we have a theme song for this production? I mean, wouldn't that be sort of neat to have at least one of the productions in this readers theatre book with its own theme song, you know, something that people would want to sing on their way to work or while they were shopping for groceries, or while they …

WILLIAM TELL: HEY! HEY! HEY! Enough already. Geez Louise. Just how the heck did you get assigned as the narrator for this story? Did you come over from the narrator's union or are you just some new person trying out for the job? It seems to me that you haven't done very many of these things before, have you?

NARRATOR: Well, sure I have. I just got my Narrator's license a few days ago. I had to do all the training and then take the test, just like all the other narrators. So I'm a bona fide and certified narrator just like all those other narrators in all those other readers theatre scripts in the book.

WILLIAM TELL: (*irritated*) Hey, look, to be perfectly honest, we're really not interested in your life story here. All you need to do is set up the story and let us professional actors take it from there. O.K.? So let's cool it with all the chatter and get on with the action. O.K.?

NARRATOR: Gee, O.K. You don't have to be so sensitive about it.

WILLIAM TELL: (*more irritated*) A-n-y t-i-m-e!

NARRATOR: O.K. So, where was I? Oh, yeah, see once upon a time in merry old England . . .

WILLIAM TELL: Now, hold on just a minute here, Narrator person. First of all, this story didn't just take place "once upon a time." It actually took place in the fourteenth century. And, it didn't happen in merry old England. It happened in Switzerland.

NARRATOR: Switzerland?

WILLIAM TELL: Yes, Switzerland!

NARRATOR:	Not "once upon a time" time?
WILLIAM TELL:	(*exasperated*) Right! Not "once upon a time" time. So, can we get on with the story, now?
NARRATOR:	(*checking the script*) O.K., I think I've got it now. So, according to the version of the story I have right here there was this really evil ruler from the country of Austria. He was so evil that he made everyone throughout the land salute his hat—that's right, everyone had to salute the ruler's hat.
EVIL RULER:	Hey, Narrator person, if you're not careful, we might just accidentally on purpose lose you from this story.
NARRATOR:	Hey, hold on. All I'm doing is reading from the script they gave me. Don't blame me if the story hasn't been written the way you would like it to be written. I'm just doing a job here and it seems as though everybody in this story wants to tell me how to do this job. Remember, I'm a certified and licensed professional narrator (*with a sweeping hand*). So everybody, just ease off. O.K.? Let's just do the story, say our parts, and we'll all be nice happy campers. Okeydokey?
EVIL RULER:	Fine, but just remember that I'm watching you.
NARRATOR:	(*sarcastically*) Yeah, right! (*more forcefully*) So, as I was saying, this evil ruler person made everyone salute his hat whenever he walked by. Everyone did, 'cause they were all afraid of him and all that. And besides, because his name was Evil Ruler everyone figured that he might do something really really terrible. . . .
EVIL RULER:	(*slowly*) I'm watching you.
NARRATOR:	(*after a furtive glance at the Evil Ruler*) So, anyway, everyone salutes the hat . . . everyone, that is, except William Tell. This gets the Evil Ruler really upset. How dare he (William Tell) not salute my hat, the Evil Ruler mumbles to himself. Now, before our Evil Ruler person here gets ticked

off at me I want to let you know that rulers, whether they are evil or not, don't necessarily do a lot of mumbling. I mean, it's not like they have nothing better to do with their time. After all, being a ruler is a lot of work. And particularly if you are an evil ruler, which requires a lot more work than those regular average type rulers that you find in some of those European countries. . . .

WILLIAM TELL: (*loudly at narrator*) Hey, you! Yeah, you! Look, I don't know whether you realize it or not, but you sure do a lot of rambling. Where did you say you went to narrator's school? Come on, how 'bout getting with the program here. It's the characters who are supposed to be doing most of the talking, not the narrator. Your job is simply to introduce the characters and move the action along at strategic points in the story. (*getting upset*) So, enough of this mindless chatter, O.K.? Just get on with the story.

NARRATOR: First it was the Evil Ruler person who gives me grief with all those threats and stuff. And now, it's the major character who thinks he owns this whole production and can just tell anybody he wants how this production should be run. They never told us about this in narrator's school, but it's really starting to get me ticked off.

WILLIAM TELL: Hey, we're sorry we're getting you upset. We know it's your first day on the job, but all we're asking is for you to just do your job the way you were trained to do it. O.K.?

NARRATOR: O.K.

EVIL RULER: (*impatiently*) And you better do it fast. Just take a look (*points to script*). See that? That means that the writer is running out of ideas and the story's about to end. So, what do you say we get this thing moving? And, real fast.

NARRATOR: O.K. O.K. So, as I was saying, William Tell wouldn't salute the Evil Ruler's hat. (*faster*) So, the Evil Ruler ordered him to shoot an apple off his son's head. He shot the apple off the son's head, and then told the Evil Ruler that if he had missed and killed his son, he would have turned around and killed the Evil Ruler himself. (*rapidly*) Well, this really got the Evil Ruler upset and so the Evil Ruler put our hero, William Tell, in a deep dark dungeon that was filled with all kinds of slimy creatures and William Tell vowed that he would escape from the prison and come and get the Evil Ruler and then one day William Tell . . .

WRITER: (*exasperated and completely frustrated*) Sorry to interrupt folks, but that's all the time we have for this story.

NARRATOR: And they all lived happily ever after.

Johnny Kumquatseed Walks Along the Road of Life and Gets a Job and (Thankfully) a New Name

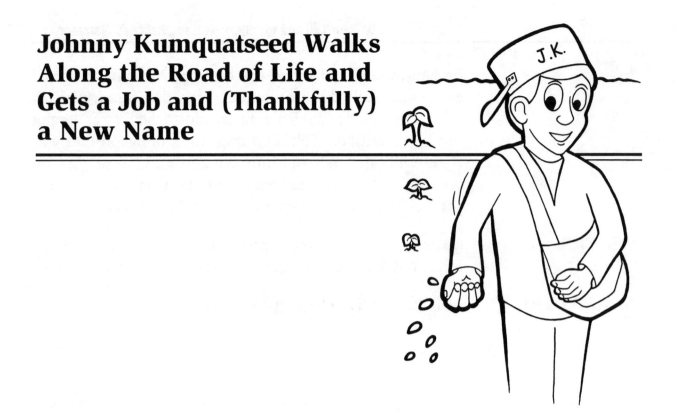

STAGING: The narrator can be standing or positioned behind a lectern or podium. The "Offstage Voice" can be positioned anywhere in the room. The Persons Along The Road Of Life can be sitting on tall stools. Johnny can walk from person to person as the production unfolds.

Person 3 Along The Road Of Life
           X

                  Person 2 Along The Road Of Life
                            X

                                  Person 1 Along The Road Of Life
                                            X

                                                  Johnny
                                                    X

Narrator
X

                                                  (Offstage Voice)
                                                    X

NARRATOR:	Long ago on the American frontier, there lived a young boy by the name of Johnny Kumquatseed. Now, you may think that Johnny's name was very unusual, but just remember that this story took place during the "Good Old Days" when people weren't as original or creative as they are now. In fact, parents back then didn't have any idea what to name their kids and often they would name their children after things they found around the house. Well, as it happens, when Johnny was born his father had just bought a load of kumquats to feed the family.
OFFSTAGE VOICE:	Hey, what the heck are kumquats?
NARRATOR:	Well, kumquats are actually native to China and Indochina and are members of the citrus family. The fruits grow on small evergreen shrubs and are about as large as a small plum. Cultivated extensively in the Orient, they are very sweet to the taste. There are two species of kumquats: the round kumquat and the oval kumquat. Kumquats make up the genus *Fortunella* of the family . . .
OFFSTAGE VOICE:	O.K., O.K., we get the picture!
NARRATOR:	Well, anyway, when Johnny was born he was named after the first thing his father saw in the house.
OFFSTAGE VOICE:	It's good thing his father didn't notice the smelly pig pen when Johnny was born! Ha, ha, ha, ha, ha!
NARRATOR:	Hmmmmmm, now where was I? Oh, yeah. Well, as I was saying, Johnny grew up on the frontier, way out in the sticks. Pretty soon he was old enough to leave the frontier and begin to live his own life. But, now, maybe I should turn the story over to our hero, Johnny.
JOHNNY:	Thanks, Narrator person. And so, as my friend was saying, I left home to seek my fortune in the world. It was only when I got out into the world that I discovered something really interesting—I had a really strange name. Now, in most cases, I wouldn't have minded, but I really wanted to

be someone important like the president of the United States or the head of Microsoft® or something important like that. But, as I discovered, people tended to look at my name instead of the individual behind the name. Let me show you what I mean.

PERSON 1 ALONG THE ROAD OF LIFE:	Hey, young man, I see you're walking along the road of life seeking your fame and fortune and making a name for yourself. By the way, what IS your name?
JOHNNY:	My name is Johnny Kumquatseed.
PERSON 1 ALONG THE ROAD OF LIFE:	Hmmmmmm. That's certainly a strange and unusual name. I do know how you got that name because I was listening to the Narrator explain it earlier in this story. But don't you think that name will hinder your progress along the road of life?
JOHNNY:	I'm really not sure. I've never been on the road of life before, but I'm willing to give it a shot.
PERSON 1 ALONG THE ROAD OF LIFE:	Well, good luck. You'll need it!
NARRATOR:	And so it was that Johnny continued his journey along the road of life. Pretty soon he was in Pennsylvania, where he met another person.
PERSON 2 ALONG THE ROAD OF LIFE:	Howdy, stranger. Are you just passing through or are you planning to stay for a spell?
JOHNNY:	No, just passing through. I'm out to seek my fortune along the road of life.
PERSON 2 ALONG THE ROAD OF LIFE:	Well, if I can offer some friendly advice, I think you're really going to find it tough out there. I, too, was listening to the narrator of your story so I know what your name is. And, to be perfectly honest, I think that that name will cause you all kinds of grief along the way.

JOHNNY:	Well, I appreciate the concern, but I want to give it a shot nonetheless.
PERSON 2 ALONG THE ROAD OF LIFE:	Good luck to you, young man. You'll certainly need it.
NARRATOR:	Just about now, Johnny was beginning to wonder about his name. He was beginning to have some second thoughts. But he decided to continue his journey down the road of life. He was now in Indiana and he was getting very tired from his travels. It was there that he met Person 3 Along The Road Of Life.
PERSON 3 ALONG THE ROAD OF LIFE:	Well, young man, I certainly know who you are simply because I've been paying attention to the entire story and I'm going to offer you the best advice ever. First of all, before you go anywhere else along this here road of life you're definitely going to need a job. I mean, after all, you just can't walk your way through story after story and expect that all the other characters in those stories will support you. If you're going to be anything at all, you need to get a job and then you need to get a life.
JOHNNY:	You mean, I'm going to have to work for a living?
PERSON 3 ALONG THE ROAD OF LIFE:	That's absolutely correct. It's one thing to be a perpetual story character—just look at Cinderella or Red Riding Hood or Paul Bunyan. What kind of future do they have? All they can do is act in a story or two and that's about it. They are perpetual story characters. But I know you want to be something more. You want to make a contribution to society! You want to make a difference!
JOHNNY:	You bet, Person 3 Along The Road Of Life! I want to be somebody! I want to be me! (*breaks into song—for example, tune from "Man of La Mancha"*) I gotta be me! I gotta be me! For once in my life, I gotta be me!

PERSON 3 ALONG THE ROAD OF LIFE:	You're absolutely right, Johnny. (*forcefully*) And the best way you can be you is to get THAT job and take your place as a productive working member of society.
JOHNNY:	(*proudly and boldly*) You're right! YOU'RE ABSOLUTELY RIGHT!
NARRATOR:	And so it was that Johnny got that job. And that job involved harvesting apples in the state of Washington. (After all, it was a very long road of life that Johnny had been walking on.) And Johnny became the BEST apple harvester in the entire country. (*louder and more boldly*) And men looked up to him! And women looked up to him! And children looked up to him! He was a hero . . . a bona fide hero . . . a true blue AMERICAN HERO! (*strong and powerful*) He WAS Johnny Kumquatseed—AN AMERICAN HERO.
OFFSTAGE VOICE:	(*whispering*) Hey, Narrator person, aren't you forgetting something? What about that name?
NARRATOR:	Oh, yeah, I almost forgot. It was years later, as Johnny's story was told around campfires all across the frontier, that somebody—we don't know who—accidentally referred to Johnny as Johnny Appleseed because he spent his life with apples. And it was from that time to the present day that we have known him as Johnny Appleseed . . . Johnny Appleseed—AMERICAN HERO!
OFFSTAGE VOICE:	It's a good thing that the person who made that mistake didn't accidentally sit on a very thorny desert plant. Just imagine if we knew our hero as . . . as . . . as Johnny Cactusbutt.

The Last Story in This Section of the Book

Staging: The narrator can be placed on a tall stool or be standing to one side of the staging area. The characters should be walking around throughout the presentation.

Peter Pan	Town Mouse			
X	X			
	Gingerbread Man		Pinocchio	
	X		X	
		Cinderella		John Henry
		X		X
Narrator				Teacher
X				X

NARRATOR: Once upon a . . .

PETER PAN: (*interrupting*) Hey, hold it just a minute, buddy.

NARRATOR: What's the problem?

PETER PAN: (*irritated*) Look, I've been looking at all the stories in this readers theatre book this class has been using. There are stories about frogs, and princesses, and giant people, and dragons, and all those other story characters. But not once, not even one little time, is there a story about me.

TOWN MOUSE:	You know, you're absolutely right, Peter. I looked around too and do you think there's a story somewhere in this book about me? Noooooooooooooooooooooooooooo!
NARRATOR:	(*calming*) Hey, keep your shirts on.
GINGERBREAD BOY:	(*angry*) Hey, you guys are right! I would think that of all the really interesting characters in storyland, the writer would have, at least, included me. But, guess what? I'm not in any story. Now, I'm starting to get ticked!
NARRATOR:	Whoa, slow down guys.
PINOCCHIO:	(*mad*) Yeah, right! You know, come to think of it, the writer never included me in any story—not in this book, not in the first book, and not in the second book. Ohhhhhh, boy, that really stinks. After all the pleasure I've been giving kids all these years. And let's not mention that really neat movie the folks over at Disney did on my life.
NARRATOR:	Hey, this is getting entirely out of hand. You guys have just got to settle down. There must be some logical explanation here somewhere.
CINDERELLA:	(*angrily*) Explanation, Shmecksplanation! I can't believe what I'm seeing. Who does that writer think he is? Aren't I one of the loveliest and most beautiful story characters that ever appeared in a book? I mean, kids have been reading about me for years. But, do you think that writer has one brain cell large enough to think about including me in his book? (*shakes her fist*) Oh, boy, just wait till I get my hands on him!
JOHN HENRY:	(*frustrated*) Hey, this guy must be a real jerk! Aren't I one of the strongest characters in any American folktale? And where does he put me? NOWHERE, that's where. Not a single word! Not a single page! Not a single story! Nothing! It's obvious this writer person doesn't know diddly squat.
NARRATOR:	Hey, guys let's settle down.

PETER PAN:	(*really angry*) Settle down, are you kidding? This writer person, whoever he may be, has just slighted some of the most powerful and most memorable story characters in all of literature.
TOWN MOUSE:	(*really mad*) Yeah, who does he think he is? Here we are, waiting around for some decent story so we can do our parts, and he goes off writing tales about salamanders and fairy godmothers and that Goldilocks character again.
GINGERBREAD BOY:	(*loudly*) WHAT A JERK! WHAT A JERK!
NARRATOR:	Whoa, this is getting way out of hand.
PINOCCHIO:	(*very mad*) Step aside, Narrator person. We're taking over now. I think we've all about had it up to here with that writer guy and his weird ideas. He's probably in it just for the money. Yeah, that's probably it. He thinks he can just write a couple of stories with some minor characters, print them up in some book, sell those books to teachers all over the country, and then retire to some condo in Hawaii with his lovely wife and a BMW. And what happens to us? Nothing! That's what!
CINDERELLA:	(*fuming*) Oh, just wait till I get my hands on him. I'm going to take this glass slipper and shove it right between his . . . .
JOHN HENRY:	(*angry*) Hey, I know. Why don't we just all get together and go to his house and tell him a thing or two? What do you say, guys? Are you ready?
ALL:	Yes, yes, yes! (*They all storm offstage.*)
NARRATOR:	(*somewhat dejectedly*) Well, there you have it. Just as I was trying to tell you guys a really nice story all the characters just up and left me. (*now excitedly*) Hey, wait a minute, I think I've got an idea. Why don't you guys try and save the writer?
AUDIENCE:	How, oh wise and really cool Narrator person?

NARRATOR:	(*excitedly*) Easy! All you need to do is create your own versions of fairy tales and legends and folktales and tall tales and other kinds of stories into readers theatre scripts. And be sure to use one or more of the leftover characters that the writer of this book didn't use. Then, you'll have some really neat stories you can share with other students in the school, you'll save the life of the writer of this book before those story characters (*points to exiting characters*) catch up with him at his house, and, who knows, maybe people will want to buy your stories and then you can retire to that condo in Hawaii. The characters are all included, you save the life of the writer, and maybe you all make lots of money in the process.
AUDIENCE:	Wow, what a really neat idea!
TEACHER:	I think it's a terrific idea! What do you say? Let's go!

Part III

OH BOY, OH BOY, A BUNCH OF STORIES ABOUT
SALAMANDERS

The Ugly Salamander (or the Bad-Looking Creature Gets Involved with a Very Large Family)

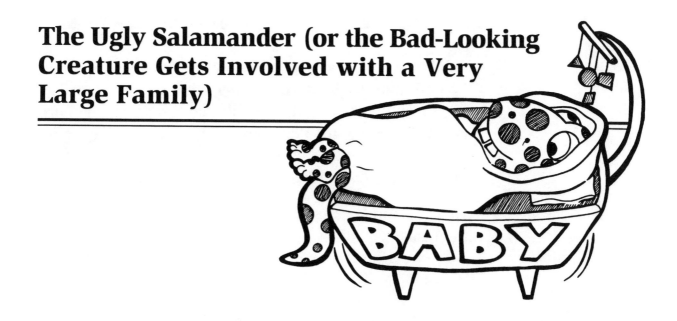

STAGING: The narrator can be standing or placed behind a podium or lectern. All the other characters can be seated in chairs.

Mama Frog   Papa Frog   Baby Salamander
X   X   X

Offstage Voice
X

Narrator
X

NARRATOR: Once upon a time there lived this happy family of frogs. There was Papa Frog . . .

PAPA FROG: Hi, there.

NARRATOR: There was Mama Frog . . .

MAMA FROG: Hi, there!

NARRATOR: And there were about 1,234,567 baby frogs, but we won't ask each of them to say "Hi" to you.

Anyway, the frog family lived on the edge of a pond somewhere in a land far away from here. They were a very happy family and always enjoyed doing typical frog things. The

93

children would always play "Leapfrog," Mama Frog would hop around the pond getting her chores done, and Papa Frog would just sit on his log all day and croak and burp, croak and burp, croak and burp. But, then, one day something really strange and unusual happened. But I think I'd better let Mama and Papa tell you themselves.

PAPA FROG:　　Hey, Narrator person, when did we suddenly get this ability to speak just like you human being persons? After all, we're frogs and all frogs are good for is going "Ribbit, ribbit, ribbit."

NARRATOR:　　Well, you see, through the miracle of imagination and a very wise writer, we have been able to give you several human qualities. For example, not only are you able to talk like a human being person, but you're also able to sit on a chair. Now, how many frogs in the real world do you know who can do that?

PAPA FROG:　　You're right, not many.

MAMA FROG:　　But, what if we don't want all these human being person qualities? What if all we want to be is just your everyday common average frogs in a pond? After all, this is the way we lived for thousands of years; why should we change now?

NARRATOR:　　Well, if it were up to me I wouldn't change you at all. But you see, there was this writer person who wanted to create a story about an ugly salamander—and why he chose an ugly salamander as the hero of a children's story I'll never know.

MAMA FROG:　　Hey, wait a gosh-darn minute here. I thought this was going to be a story about our happy little frog family. How did some gross and disgusting salamander get into this story?

NARRATOR:　　To be honest, I have actually no idea. Again, it's that writer person who wrote the story and for some reason he thought it would be neat to lead it off with you guys. I mean you're all good looking . . . you're bright . . . you're well educated . . . you live in a good neighborhood . . . well, anyway I think you get the picture.

PAPA FROG: You know, Mama, our friendly Narrator person does have a point. We are an ideal family and I can see why the author person wanted to begin his story with us. I just hope he doesn't forget about us later—especially when he brings in that stupid salamander character. You know how salamanders are—they want to hog all the action and tell everybody what to do. We'll just have to keep our big bulging eyes on him.

NARRATOR: O.K., you two ready now?

PAPA FROG & (*together*) Yeah!
MAMA FROG:

NARRATOR: O.K., getting back to our story. One day Mama Frog had just laid about 67,901 eggs along the edge of the pond. Papa Frog was so proud that he was passing out cigars to all the herons and snakes and storks that lived around the pond. Mama and Papa carefully watched their eggs and guarded them from any and all predators, you know, like those funny looking lizards from across the pond.

Anyway, one day all the eggs started hatching. One by one tiny little tadpoles began popping out of the eggs . . . dozens, hundreds, thousands. The whole place was covered by these little cute tadpoles . . . EXCEPT, for one very strange creature! For there, right in the middle of these thousands and thousands of froglets was a very strange and very ugly baby.

SALAMANDER Hey, careful there. You know, salamanders have feelings,
BABY: too.

NARRATOR: Sorry, I guess I just got carried away.

MAMA FROG:	Well, as our Narrator person was saying, there was this really weird looking baby in the midst of all our other babies.
PAPA FROG:	So, we said, "How the heck did that ugly thing get there?"
NARRATOR:	Well, because none of the other animals could speak or much less understand English, Mama and Papa Frog didn't get an answer.
PAPA FROG:	So, what do you think, Narrator person?
NARRATOR:	I'm not allowed to think. The writer just put me into this story to move the action along. I'm just following orders: saying my assigned parts, giving you guys an opportunity to talk like real live human being persons, and basically minding my own business.
MAMA FROG:	In other words, the only reason you're in this story in the first place is simply because the writer put you in the story.
NARRATOR:	That's about it!
MAMA FROG:	Well, O.K., might as well get on with the rest of the story.
NARRATOR:	So, Mama and Papa carefully watched. And before too long, out came a tiny baby salamander.
BABY SALAMANDER:	That's me!
NARRATOR:	Mama and Papa frog were very surprised. (*points to a member of the audience*) Wouldn't you be surprised if your mother went to the hospital to have a baby and came home carrying a baby salamander?
MAMA FROG:	Hey, let's get on with it. I'm looking ahead here and see that this story is just about ready to end. We need to pick up the action here, narrator person.
NARRATOR:	Hey, just hold on to your big bulging eyes. I'm moving as fast as I can.

BABY SALAMANDER:	And don't forget, I've got to be finished with this story in time for me to leave this aquatic environment and move to a more terrestrial environment.
NARRATOR:	(*slightly irritated*) O.K., O.K., O.K. I'll pick it up. So, as I was saying, Papa and Mama noticed that the ugly baby was very different from all the other 67,900 babies in the pond. But being the loving and caring couple that they were, they decided to care for this strange and unusual baby just like he was one of their own. They fed him, washed him, kept the predators away, and even changed his diaper several times a day. He grew and grew and grew just like all his "sisters" and "brothers." He was just like all his siblings except that he was so much uglier than them. And then, something really strange happened.
OFFSTAGE VOICE:	What? What? What?
NARRATOR:	Our really weird baby went through metamorphosis and changed into an adult salamander.
OFFSTAGE VOICE:	And he became the most beautiful creature in the entire pond?
NARRATOR:	No, unfortunately, he was still a salamander, which meant that he was still very ugly. I'm sorry, but this story doesn't have a happy ending like all those fairy tales you've heard. This is just real life. Baby salamanders and adult salamanders are both pretty ugly . . . that's just the way it is . . . it's a fact of life . . . get over it and move on.
BABY SALAMANDER:	Yeah, but at least I don't have to spend the rest of my life snatching flies out of the air with an over-sized tongue like (*points to frogs*) all my so-called relatives.

The Salamander Prince

STAGING: The narrator stands in back and to the side of the other characters. The princes can be on tall stools or seated in chairs. They may use a toy telephone for their conversation with the writer.

```
        Narrator
           X

                        Really Handsome Prince
                                 X

                                    Really Good-Looking Prince
                                                X

          Really Dashing Prince
                   X

                           Somewhat Balding Author in Pennsylvania
                                           X
```

REALLY HANDSOME PRINCE:	Hey, just a gosh-darn minute here. I just took a look at the title of this story and noticed that it's about some salamander prince. Hey, what the heck is a salamander prince?
REALLY GOOD-LOOKING PRINCE:	Yeah, what gives? How come the writer made up a story about some weird salamander? Didn't he know that all these stories should have really good-looking characters in them?

REALLY DASHING PRINCE:	Yeah, and what do you think the prince's union is going to say about all of this? I mean, when they find out that a Somewhat Balding Author in Pennsylvania has created a story with a salamander prince as the lead character then they're really going to be ticked off.
REALLY HANDSOME PRINCE:	(*indignantly*) THEY'RE GOING TO BE TICKED OFF!!! What about us? If authors begin letting every Tom, Dick, and Salamander into the stories they write then we're going to be out of a job.
REALLY GOOD-LOOKING PRINCE:	And that's not all. What about all those really beautiful princesses? Before you know it, the salamanders will start getting the good scenes with the princesses. And what will we be doing? Probably just mumbling in the background.
REALLY DASHING PRINCE:	You know what? I think we'd better get hold of that Somewhat Balding Author in Pennsylvania and tell him a thing or two.
NARRATOR:	And, so, the Really Handsome Prince and the Really Good-Looking Prince and the Really Dashing Prince began surfing the Internet to locate the Somewhat Balding Author in Pennsylvania to ask him why he titled a story "The Salamander Prince." They soon discovered that the writer had his own Web site and before long they were on the phone with him.
REALLY HANDSOME PRINCE:	(*talking on the telephone*) Hey, writer man, what gives? What's this about drafting a story with some sort of salamander prince as the lead character?
SOMEWHAT BALDING AUTHOR IN PENNSYLVANIA:	Hey, guys, how are you doing? It's been a long time. How's life down at the castle? And how's the Missus? It's great to hear your voices again.
REALLY GOOD-LOOKING PRINCE:	What do you say we cut the chitchat? Let's get to the meat of the matter. How come you gave some salamander dude top billing over us?

SOMEWHAT BALDING AUTHOR IN PENNSYLVANIA:	Well, guys, it's like this. You see I've been including all of you in all the other stories I've written. I mean, look at all the parts you guys got in the *Frantic Frogs and Other Frankly Fractured Folktales for Readers Theatre* book I wrote several years ago. And you must agree that the leading roles I wrote for you three in the other book, *Tadpole Tales and Other Totally Terrific Treats for Readers Theatre*, made you stars. Don't you remember all the letters you three got from ladies all over the country?
REALLY DASHING PRINCE:	Yeah, that was kinda cool. After all, we did get lots of attention and a few movie offers thanks to the stuff you wrote for us.
SOMEWHAT BALDING AUTHOR IN PENNSYLVANIA:	And not only that, you each got your own agent and publicist and you were all featured on the cover of Teen Beat magazine and fan clubs started up all over and you began appearing on all the talk shows and, well, I think you get the idea. In short, you got lots of attention as a result of those stories.
REALLY HANDSOME PRINCE:	You know guys, he's right. We have gotten lots of publicity and attention.
REALLY GOOD-LOOKING PRINCE:	Yeah, I guess so. I mean if it hadn't been for our friend the Somewhat Balding Author in Pennsylvania, where would we be now? Probably just sitting around some dingy castle waiting for some drop-dead gorgeous princess to discover us.
REALLY DASHING PRINCE:	I guess you're right. We do owe you a lot. You made us the Really Handsome, Really Good-Looking, and Really Dashing Princes we are today.
SOMEWHAT BALDING AUTHOR IN PENNSYLVANIA:	Hey, no problem, guys. Glad to do it. But I also thought it might be a good idea to bring in some new characters once in awhile. You know, sort of spread the wealth around, you might say. So, being the creative type, I thought it might be a good idea to give our salamander friend a juicy role, if

you know what I mean. Besides, he's worked hard in all the other stories in the book and it was time for his starring role.

REALLY HANDSOME PRINCE: Well, I think you're right.

REALLY GOOD-LOOKING PRINCE: I concur.

REALLY DASHING PRINCE: Then we're all agreed. Our friend, the Somewhat Balding Author in Pennsylvania, can go ahead and write a story about a salamander prince. Good luck, Somewhat Balding Author!

NARRATOR: And so it was that the Somewhat Balding Author in Pennsylvania wrote the title for a new readers theatre script called "The Salamander Prince." Now all he needed to do was to write the whole story. But then, that's another story. Or, that's another story about another story. Or, er, that's a story about a story that's about another story. Ah, er, ah, or it's a story about another story that's not this story but another story about how the story that was not about this story got a title but didn't have a story about its story yet. I think. Never mind, I think you know the story.

The Big Bad Salamander and the Three Little Pigs

STAGING: The narrator can stand to the front of the staging area and then leave quickly. The other characters can sit on stools or chairs arranged haphazardly around the staging area.

Well-Known Author		World Famous Scientist
X		X
	Big Bad Salamander	
	X	
Youngest Pig	Middle-Aged Pig	Oldest Pig
X	X	X
		Narrator
		X

NARRATOR: You know, to be honest with you, I'm not sure why I'm in this story. You'll be able to understand and enjoy this story perfectly well without me around to muck things up. So, if you don't mind, I think I'll just take the day off and go to the beach. Bye, see ya! (*leaves*)

WELL-KNOWN AUTHOR: O.K., now it's my turn. You see this story takes place in a magical time in a magical place with some pretty magical characters. And here's how it goes. You see, once upon a time there were these three pigs who wanted to be independent and all that stuff and so they set out to each build a house.

YOUNGEST PIG: O.K., guys, I'm the youngest pig and as a result I'm not worldly wise. So I think I'll just build my house of straw.

MIDDLE-AGED PIG: O.K., I'm the middle child. I'm wiser than my younger brother, but not quite as smart as my older sibling. So I think I'll just build my house of sticks.

OLDEST PIG: O.K., I'm the oldest brother in this bunch, which means that I'm probably the wisest one of all. So I'll just build my little cottage out of bricks.

WELL-KNOWN AUTHOR: So, as you can see, each of the three brothers built his own house, one of straw (pretty dumb), one of sticks (not entirely bright), and one of bricks (pretty cool, huh?). Now, as you know, we need an evil character in these kinds of stories, so let's bring him in: the Big Bad Salamander.

BIG BAD SALAMANDER: Heeeeeeeeeeeeeeey! I'm the big bad salamander and I'm mean and nasty and cruel and evil and all that other stuff. And I'm going to visit each one of the three pig's houses and blow each one of them down. I don't know why I'm blowing them down, but that's just the way it is in these stories and I'm just trying to earn an honest buck.

WELL-KNOWN AUTHOR: So the big bad salamander strolled on over to the first little pig's house.

BIG BAD SALAMANDER: Little Pig, Little Pig, let me in,
I have a nasty temper and an evil grin.
I'm big and I'm mean and full of fright,
And I'll eat you up all day and night.

YOUNGEST PIG: Oh no, oh no, oh no. Not by the hairs of my chinny chin chin!

WELL-KNOWN AUTHOR: And so the Big Bad Salamander huffed and puffed and blew the Youngest Pig's house down. And before long he was feasting on some really good pork chops.

WORLD FAMOUS SCIENTIST: Hey, just a gosh-darn minute here. This whole story just doesn't make any sense.

MIDDLE-AGED PIG:	What do you mean, oh World Famous Scientist?
OLDEST PIG:	Don't tell me that you're going to mess up our story by telling us that it's scientifically inaccurate.
WORLD FAMOUS SCIENTIST:	That's just it. It's all wrong. What are all those boys and girls out there in storyland going to think if a bunch of storybook characters can't get their scientific information correct? They're simply not going to believe anything you say. You'll lose all your credibility with them and every other story will come under suspicion.
WELL-KNOWN AUTHOR:	(*indignantly*) Oh, that's just great. Just what we need is some smarty-pants scientist type who thinks she knows everything and has to mess with our cute little story just so it can be scientifically accurate.
WORLD FAMOUS SCIENTIST:	Hey, don't blame me. It's all those boys and girls who will begin to wonder about every other story you write if you can't make this story right.
WELL-KNOWN AUTHOR:	So, what do you suggest, Miss I've-Got-An-I.Q.-Bigger-Than-The-Grand-Canyon?
WORLD FAMOUS SCIENTIST:	Well, first I think you need to know that salamanders don't normally eat pigs. Their diet consists primarily of worms, slugs, snails, and other small creatures.
WELL-KNOWN AUTHOR:	(*perturbed*) Oh, that's just fine and dandy. Now we're going to have a story where our main character goes around to some slug's house and huffs and puffs his way through that place.
WORLD FAMOUS SCIENTIST:	I'm afraid that won't work either. You see most salamanders breathe through their skin and there is even one group of salamanders known as the lungless salamanders, which have completely lost their lungs and are incapable of huffing or puffing or anything like that.

WELL-KNOWN AUTHOR:	(*more indignant*) Oh, this is just great. Now you'll tell me that our salamander friend won't be able to visit the pig's houses at all. Right?
WORLD FAMOUS SCIENTIST:	I'm afraid you're right. You see, salamanders are somewhat sluggish and shy. And besides, they require moisture and like to spend their days in wet habitats such as swamps or rainforests or other watery environments.
WELL-KNOWN AUTHOR:	(*really upset*) Oh, this is just great. I've put together a really cool story for all the kids and you come along and throw a wet blanket, so to speak, over the whole operation. Now, what am I going to do?
YOUNGEST PIG:	Yeah, what are we going to do?
MIDDLE-AGED PIG:	Yeah, what are we going to do?
OLDEST PIG:	Well, because I'm the oldest and wisest, I guess it's going to be up to me to save the day. (*to author*) It just seems as though you're going to have to change your main character. It's quite obvious that it can't be a salamander because the story wouldn't be scientifically accurate. So what you need is some mean and ugly character that makes a lot of noise, but isn't very bright. A character that won't have as many lines as we do. One who's full of hot air. One who's about as dumb as a doornail. One who's . . .
WELL-KNOWN AUTHOR:	(*excitedly*) Hey, I've got it. How about a wolf? A wolf would be perfect. They're ugly and they make a lot of noise and they've got lungs they can use to huff and puff and they would be easy to draw for anybody doing the illustrations for the book. Wow, this is great. Just give me a few days and I'll be able to make the changes and we'll be right back to our story.

BIG BAD SALAMANDER: And that's how I got left out of the final version of the story. I lost my job and had to go on unemployment. I returned to the swamp and crawled under a big wet pile of leaves. I sulked and I cried. And, I DIDN'T live happily ever after.

AUDIENCE: Awwwwwwwwwwwwww!

A Story About a Really Dumb Prince Who Doesn't Know the Difference Between Salamanders and Frogs

STAGING: The narrator stands in back and to the side of the other characters. The other characters may stand or may sit on high stools.

Really Dumb Prince	Wicked Witch	Salamander 1	Salamander 2
X	X	X	X
			Narrator
			X

NARRATOR: Once upon a time there was this really dumb prince who lived in a very large castle by a big cruddy swamp filled with funny green amphibians. Now, you should know that this prince was probably the dumbest of the dumb. How dumb, you might ask? He was so dumb that he couldn't find his own head if he used both hands. He was so dumb that he thought that if he could get any amphibian to kiss him then he would become enchanted and would be able to marry the richest and most beautiful woman in the kingdom. I mean, that's really dumb. But I'm getting ahead of my own story. Let's look in on this really dumb prince and some of the really dumb things he does. As you might expect, our story begins in the swamp.

REALLY DUMB PRINCE: (*slowly*) Well, here I am again sitting on this lily pad. I sure do hope some enchanted amphibian comes along to kiss me so we can live happily ever after.

WICKED WITCH: (*shouting*) Hey, Prince!

REALLY DUMB PRINCE: (*confused*) Say, where did you come from?

WICKED WITCH: Hey, you can't really be *THAT* dumb. You know there's always some kind of wicked witch in stories like these. We just happen to be there.

REALLY DUMB PRINCE: (*slowly, thoughtfully*) Yeah, now I remember. That must mean that you've got a whole pocket full of evil spells and magic sayings. How about tossing one my way?

WICKED WITCH: Now, why would I want to waste a spell on a really dumb prince? If I'm going to put a spell on anyone, at least it's going to be on a prince with some smarts. After all, I've got a reputation to maintain. If I cast a magic spell on every prince I meet then there's no telling how many enchanted creatures we'd have hopping around these stories. Say, why do you want a spell, anyway?

REALLY DUMB PRINCE: Oh, I don't really want a spell. What I want is to have you cast a spell on one of these lovely critters in the swamp so that when I kiss it, it will turn into some lovely princess that I can carry off into "Happily Ever After" Land.

SALAMANDER 1: (*defiantly*) Now hold on just a minute, buster! Don't you have your story lines confused? It's those frog types that you want to kiss. Just because we're amphibians like those frogs creatures doesn't mean you can go around kissing any slimy creature you want to. Hey, we've got a life to live, too.

SALAMANDER 2: (*defiantly*) Yeah! And, besides, how were you planning on kissing us anyway? We don't have lips, you know.

SALAMANDER 1: Wow! You're not only dumb, you're dumber than dumb! Don't you know that in every fairy tale the wicked witch just casts her spells on princes and turns them into frogs (ugh) who wait for some desperate princesses to kiss them?

WICKED WITCH: (*irritated*) Hey, just a minute. Who do you think you are, telling me who I can cast my spells on? After all, if I want to cast my spell on some slimy amphibian rather than a human being, well I'm certainly entitled to do so . . . and NO no-lipped salamander is going to tell me otherwise.

REALLY DUMB PRINCE: Wait! Are you telling me that there is a difference between frogs and salamanders? Do you mean that I've been spending my life kissing all the wrong creatures in this swamp?

SALAMANDER 1: That's right, big boy. Not only are you the dumbest thing on two feet, but you've been spending the better part of your life kissing every amphibian from one end of the swamp to the other.

SALAMANDER 2: Yeah, and boy you should see the smiles on all the newts and toads.

WICKED WITCH: Boy, YOU ARE DUMB! I don't think that I've got any kind of magic spell that can help you. In fact, I think you're beyond help. Anybody who doesn't know the difference between a frog and a salamander is in real trouble—brain-wise, that is.

REALLY DUMB PRINCE: (*confused*) Hey, now I'm getting confused. . . . I mean, really confused! Wasn't this supposed to be a story about my search for an enchanted princess? All I wanted was to find some green-eyed beauty here in the swamp who I could kiss and turn into a potential wife. Now, this whole story is turning into a biology lesson on different species of amphibians.

WICKED WITCH: Hey, you know, he's right. In fact, I don't even need to be in this story. Right now, I should be over in another story trying to get that pesky Snow White to eat a couple of poisoned apples. So, if you'll excuse me gentlemen . . . (*leaves*)

SALAMANDER 1:   I've got to go, too. It's getting close to hibernation time and I'm really getting tired. (*leaves*)

SALAMANDER 2:   Yeah, that sounds good to me, too. (*leaves*)

REALLY DUMB PRINCE: Well, I guess that leaves just you and me, Narrator. So, now what do we do?

NARRATOR: What do you mean WE? I'm out of here! (*leaves*)

REALLY DUMB PRINCE: (*to audience*) Oh, no, now what do I do? I'm the only character left. I'm so dumb I don't know what to do. Can anyone help me out? Can anyone tell me who I should kiss? Does anyone want to kiss me? Has anyone kissed a frog? Has anyone kissed a salamander? Can anyone tell me the difference between frogs and salamanders? Is anyone here a frog? Is anyone here a salamander? Can anyone tell me how this story ends? (*loudly*) Can anyone help me, P-L-E-A-S-E . . . ?

The Salamander and the Crocodile

STAGING: The narrator stands off to the side of the staging area or may sit on a tall stool. The other characters form a loose semicircle or may walk around as they are speaking.

```
                Narrator
                   X

                                   Salamander        Crocodile
                                       X                 X
                   Starter
                      X
```

NARRATOR:	Once upon a time in "Once upon a Time" time there was a salamander and a crocodile. The crocodile, because he was bigger and a reptile, thought he was the faster swimmer. The salamander, because he had a long tail and was an amphibian, thought he was the faster swimmer.
CROCODILE:	Hey, salamander, did you know that I'm the fastest creature on four feet? There is nobody who can beat me.
SALAMANDER:	Well, you do have a big mouth and bad breath, but there's no way you can match my speed.
CROCODILE:	Oh, yeah. You know, for someone who looks like a lizard and eats like a frog you sure do have a lot to say.

SALAMANDER:	Hey, look who's talking "Mr. I Look Like a Dead Log." How 'bout putting your money where your mouth is? How 'bout just you and me going one-on-one in a race around the swamp?
CROCODILE:	You're on, oh "Nocturnal One."
NARRATOR:	The crocodile and the salamander agreed to race around the swamp the next day. Announcements were posted all over the swamp inviting the other creatures to come watch the big race. Animals from near and far came to watch the big event—reptiles on one side of the swamp and amphibians on the other side—each cheering on their favorite competitor.
STARTER:	Gentlemen, the rules are as follows. You will race around the swamp one time, staying within the boundaries. You may not impede the progress of the other contestant. The first one to cross the finish line is the winner. Is that clear?
NARRATOR:	The crocodile was finishing eating his daily meal of an antelope and simply nodded his agreement. The salamander had a mouth full of flies from breakfast and so nodded his consent, too.
STARTER:	Runners take your mark. Runners get set. Go!
NARRATOR:	Both the crocodile and the salamander zoomed across the start line. (*as an aside to the audience*) Well, perhaps "zoomed" is not the correct word. Maybe I should say that they splashed or paddled or squirmed across the start line. Anyway, the crocodile slowly moved out in front of the salamander.
CROCODILE:	That little runt. Nobody beats the big guy here. I'm going to be king of the swamp once and for all.
SALAMANDER:	Oh, no. That scaly-backed reptile is getting ahead of me.

NARRATOR: The crocodile got farther and farther ahead. He made a turn at the old sunken log and headed back through the weeds near the shore. It was only a matter of time before he would win the race.

CROCODILE: Yahoo! I'm going to win.

SALAMANDER: Oh, darn! I'm going to lose.

NARRATOR: It was then that something really amazing happened—the writer got "writer's block." He didn't know how the story should end. He couldn't remember if the crocodile decided to rest for a while by the side of the swamp. He couldn't remember what happened to the salamander. He couldn't remember how the race turned out. He went completely blank.

STARTER: You mean, he forgot about me, too?

NARRATOR: Well, anyway, the writer forgot everything about the story. He was stuck and didn't know what to do. So he called his agent and asked her what could be done to end the story. The agent said that she would bring in some new writers to finish off the race. But, of course, as you know, when the new writers got through with the story they changed the crocodile into a hare and the salamander into a tortoise. Then they created this race where the hare falls sleep and the tortoise wins the race and the lesson that we all learn from this is that "slow and steady wins the race." At least, that's the movie version of the race.

CROCODILE: (*as an aside to the audience*) Of course, what our friendly neighborhood narrator can't tell you is how I devoured the salamander before he even got across the start line and the new writers had to change the whole plot so the story wouldn't upset young persons such as yourselves. But if you stick around I'll give you a great recipe for salamander stew! YUM, YUM!!

Part IV

THE PART OF THE BOOK THAT IS PRETTY CLOSE TO THE END OF THE BOOK

"Once Upon a Time"

Hey, are we having fun yet? I sure hope so! By now your students should be rolling in the aisles or doubled over with laughter and your classroom should be filled with mirth and merriment and giggles and guffaws and jocularity and joviality. (Wow, try saying that fast three times.) And, of course, your students are all saying things like, "I don't EVER want to leave fourth grade because this is THE BEST PLACE IN THE WHOLE WORLD!" and "I just love language arts so much that when I grow up and become a famous movie star I'm going to be sure my former teacher has her own condo in Hawaii and a garage filled with BMWs and a refrigerator overflowing with fine imported caviar and all the servants she could ever hope for . . . and then I'm going to do something really special for her."

Well, with all those rollicking good times filling your classroom, you're probably thinking, "Gee, how can it get any better than this?" Well, here's your friendly neighborhood author to tell you that, indeed, it can get better. In this section of the book are several stories that are designed to serve as starters for your students' own readers theatre scripts. Each of the stories in this section has been started, but not finished. Now, here's the really fun part. Invite a group of students to select one of the following "story starters" and complete it using their own ideas, plots, themes, or conclusions. Each group can add events and circumstances to a script, modify a story, or alter an idea in accordance with their own interests, logic, or warped sense of humor. Obviously, there is no right or wrong way to complete any single script; students should be encouraged to invent conclusions as they see fit. Be sure to provide sufficient opportunities for individual groups to share their completed stories with other members of the class or with other classes in your school.

INTERVIEWER: So, to what do you attribute your success?

FORMER STUDENT: I honestly believe that all my success was due to the readers theatre scripts we did in fifth grade. My teacher bought this really neat book . . . something about silly salamanders, I think . . . and she encouraged us to present the scripts to each other in the form of plays and skits.

INTERVIEWER: What were some of the things you did back then?

FORMER STUDENT: We not only put on readers theatre plays, but we were also given opportunities to create and craft our own scripts. Up until then I never realized how much fun learning could be. That teacher was a real inspiration in my life and I owe her more than I could ever express.

INTERVIEWER: So, tell us about your next project.

FORMER STUDENT: I'm writing a script on the life story of that wonderfully inspiring teacher. Financing is in place, a director has been hired, and we have several big-name actresses in mind for the lead. I want the whole world to know what she did for me and my classmates. . . . I want the whole world to learn about this extraordinary and marvelous person. . . . I want them to see her beauty and her inspiration on a thousand movie screens across America. . . . I want everyone to celebrate her magnificence as I and my classmates have ever since that fateful year several years ago.

INTERVIEWER: And what about the author of that *Silly Salamanders* book?

FORMER STUDENT: I dunno, who's he?

The Big Bad Pig and the Three Little Wolves

STAGING: The narrator sits on a tall stool. The three wolves and the pig should be standing.

                                        Third Wolf
                                            X

                            Second Wolf
                                X

                First Wolf
                    X

                                                    Big Bad Pig
                                                        X

    Narrator
        X

NARRATOR:	Everybody's heard the story about the three little pigs. But, have you ever heard the story about the three little wolves? Well, in this story the three little wolves leave home and begin walking in the woods. Then, something really terrible happens.
FIRST WOLF:	Hey, brothers, it looks like we're lost.
SECOND WOLF:	You're right. I guess we better all build a house for the night.

THIRD WOLF:	O.K., let's get started.
NARRATOR:	Each of the wolves goes off to hunt for materials. Now, you should know that two of the three little wolves are not as smart as your everyday average wolf. In fact, they're pretty dumb. Listen, and you'll see for yourself.
FIRST WOLF:	I'm going to build a nice three-story house out of these weeds I found by the river.
SECOND WOLF:	Are you crazy? Do you know what can happen? A big bad pig could come along and blow your house down.
THIRD WOLF:	Well, brother, what are you going to use to build your house?
SECOND WOLF:	I found thousands and thousands of dried leaves in the forest. I'm going to build an enormous house in the middle of the forest.
FIRST WOLF:	You know, you must be just as crazy as I am. Don't you know that that big, ugly, terrible pig with his incredibly bad breath could just as easily come along and blow your house down, too?
SECOND WOLF:	Gosh, maybe you're right. (*turning to the Third Little Wolf*) What are you going to do, brother?

Possible Conclusions

1. The Third Little Wolf puts a down payment on a condo in the city and never has to worry about The Big Bad Pig.

2. The Third Little Wolf moves into the enchanted castle and begins dating Cinderella.

3. The Big Bad Pig has a change of attitude and becomes the gardener for the Three Little Wolves.

4. Little Red Riding Hood comes over from another story and teaches the Big Bad Pig a thing or two.

5. Your idea.

Rip Van Winkle Sleeps and Snores and Sleeps and Snores and Eventually Becomes the Class's Science Experiment

STAGING: For this production, characters should use the names of actual students in the class. (For scripting purposes, characters have been simply designated as "A," "B," "C," and "Teacher." Invite students to contribute their own names [and yours] for these characters.) Throughout the entire production the Rip Van Winkle character snores, sometimes loudly, sometimes softly. The narrator can stand at a lectern or podium; other characters can be seated on tall stools or chairs.

```
        Rip Van Winkle
            X

                    A           B           C
                    X           X           X

                                                    Teacher
                                                      X

    Narrator
       X
```

NARRATOR: Not too long ago, in a time very similar to this time, in a school very similar to this school (in fact, it may have actually been this school), in a classroom very similar to this classroom (in fact, it may have actually been this classroom) with students very similar to these students (in fact, it may have actually been these students) with a teacher very similar to this teacher (in fact, it may have actually been this teacher), a story took place. This is a story very similar to the story that took place (in fact, it may have actually been this story).

TEACHER: O.K. group, let's put away those books and get ready for science class. I have a real neat experiment that I want to show you that you're really going to enjoy.

A: Hey, Teacher, what about Rip Van Winkle? Shouldn't he be part of this activity, too?

TEACHER: You're right. I've tried and tried to wake him up, but he doesn't seem to respond.

B: Maybe he's in hibernation. You remember the unit we did a few weeks ago about the different animals that hibernate and the reasons why they hibernate?

C: Yeah, you're right B. But remember what Teacher told us about hibernation. Some animals do it, while others, like humans, don't. So I guess we're going to have to rule out hibernation as Rip's problem.

A: Maybe he spent so much time studying for that math test last week that he's just now catching up on his sleep.

B: That's a possibility, too. But remember that other science unit on the human body we did. We learned about how much sleep the average person needs to stay healthy.

C: Maybe our friend there isn't so average. He certainly is strange!

TEACHER: Wow, this is neat. This wasn't the science activity I had planned, but this discussion is turning into a great "teachable moment." What do you say we use our friend Rip Van Winkle as our science experiment for the day?

EVERYBODY: YEAH! What a neat idea!

TEACHER: O.K., what other kinds of ideas or suggestions can you make for Rip's behavior?

A: Well, maybe we could see if his nerve endings are still responsive. I'd be happy to stick a couple of pins into his fingers and toes just to see if he's really asleep or just faking it.

B: Let's put a small mirror under his nose to see if any water vapor gets on it. That would be a good way to see if he's really sleeping or really alive.

C: Maybe we should check the pupils of his eyes. That would be a good way to see if he's still alive.

TEACHER: Hmmmmmmmmmm. I wonder what else we could do?

Possible Conclusions

1. The class decides to dissect Rip Van Winkle and donate his organs to the local hospital. Rip overhears the discussion and becomes fully awake.

2. Rip's snoring becomes very irritating to the entire class. They decide to silence him, but make a horrible mistake.

3. Rip's behavior infects the entire class and soon everybody is falling asleep, including Teacher.

4. Somebody in the class writes a story about Rip that becomes a national best-seller and is turned into a major motion picture that eventually wins the Academy Award for "Best Picture."

5. Your idea.

The Real Reason Robin Hood Lives in the Forest

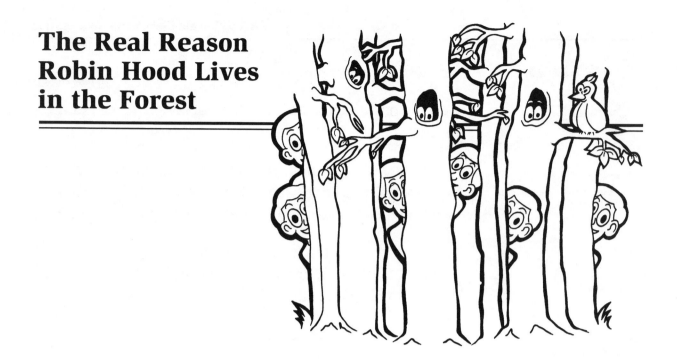

STAGING: The narrator sits on a stool off to the side of the staging area. The other characters can stand and walk around during the production or be seated on tall stools.

```
                                              Narrator
                                                 X

         Little John                  Friar Tuck
             X                            X

                      Robin Hood
                          X
```

FRIAR TUCK:　　See that Narrator person over there (*points to the narrator*). The three of us talked it over and we decided that we really didn't need a narrator for this story. We thought that the narrator would just get in the way and would mess things up by always talking. So we just decided to leave the narrator right there, but not say anything. O.K., so everybody just wave to the narrator (*the audience can wave*). Now that that's done let's get on with our story.

LITTLE JOHN:　　First of all, you have to know that our friend here (*points to Robin Hood*) is the hero of the story. And as the hero, he gets some of the best lines and, as always, he gets the beautiful princess. But because this is a "guy" story, we didn't include any women in this performance. So all of you beautiful princesses who are looking for lines to speak should probably go on over to another story if you're looking for work. We just don't have anything for you here.

FRIAR TUCK: Yeah, that's right . . . we're mean and rough and tough—we're guys!

LITTLE JOHN: YES! YES!! YES!!!

ROBIN HOOD: Hey, wait a minute. I thought that because I was the hero I would be getting all the lines. But up to this point in the story I haven't said anything. What's going on?

FRIAR TUCK: Just wait a second. This is the part of the story known as the "Setup." The author put it here so that your part would stand out and be noticed by the audience. All we get to do is talk some trash—you're the hero, remember?

ROBIN HOOD: O.K., so let's go! According to the original story I live here deep in Sherwood Forest because I and my merry band of men rob from the rich and give to the poor. But that philosophy isn't well-liked by the Sheriff of Nottingham because we're always robbing from folks around the castle.

LITTLE JOHN: That's right. And every time we rob, the sheriff chases us into the forest where we hide out and he can never find us.

ROBIN HOOD: Just a moment here, good buddy. Remember, I'm the hero of this story and I should be doing most of the talking.

LITTLE JOHN: Yeah, you're right Robin. Go ahead, I'll stay out of your way.

ROBIN HOOD: Well, as I was saying, we keep robbing and the sheriff keeps chasing us and we keep hiding in the forest and the sheriff keeps getting frustrated and so on and so on.

FRIAR TUCK: And don't forget that the king keeps getting ticked off at everything we do.

ROBIN HOOD: That's right. And somewhere in there is Maid Marian, who is probably the most beautiful woman in the world, except that we can't include her in this story because the story is an "all-guy" story. But, I digress. Actually, most people think we hide out in the forest because we're safe from the king's soldiers and the sheriff's posse, but the real reason we live in these dark dark woods is . . .

Possible Conclusions

1. Robin Hood and his band of merry men have opened a McDonald's restaurant in Sherwood Forest and are making a ton of money.

2. Robin Hood cries a lot because he never gets to spend any time with Maid Marian in this story or any other story.

3. Friar Tuck and Little John are actually professional wrestlers who secretly practice their moves in a wrestling ring in the middle of the forest.

4. Robin Hood is actually the sheriff in disguise. Little John is actually the narrator in disguise, and Friar Tuck is actually Maid Marian in disguise.

5. Your idea.

A True Story (No, Really)

STAGING: The narrator (female) stands at a podium. The other characters are seated on chairs or stools in a semicircular pattern.

```
                    Snow White        Goldy Locks
                        X                  X
          Sleep N. Beauty                      Rapunzel
                X                                  X
      Cindy Rella                                    Red Riding Hood
          X                                              X
    Narrator
        X
```

NARRATOR: Our "Once Upon a Time" story today opens up, not in some distant castle or overgrown enchanted forest, but rather in the living room of Ms. Cindy Rella. You see, Cindy is a former storybook character who got tired of the daily grind of always having to get dressed up and always having to go to some stupid ball and always having to dance with some stupid prince with the intelligence of a sack of potatoes and always having to chase after some coach that looked more like a pumpkin than a Corvette and so on and so on . . . I think you get the picture by now. Anyway, Cindy and several of her friends decided to retire from the storybook business and move out to Mother Goose Estates and away from all the big bad wolves, evil stepmothers, and princes who couldn't dance their way out of a paper bag.

And so as we begin our tale, Cindy and several of her fellow storybook companions are sitting in her living room talking about the "good old days."

GOLDY LOCKS: Hey, Cindy. Tell me, why did you finally decide to give up all that castle stuff and retire to the Estates?

CINDY: Well, you see I just got fed up with the same plot line over and over again. After all, what was I doing with my life? Every time someone would tell my story I would have to go out and work for an evil stepmother and then have a fairy godmother come and give me a beautiful Ralph Lauren original dress and get into this ugly pumpkin coach to take me to some distant palace where I would have to dance with every handsome dude, excuse me, I mean prince in the place and then lose my shoes so some out-of-work prince could try and make me believe I'd be the happiest woman around if he could just hold my feet and make me try on some old smelly slippers he always carried around with him. I don't know about you, but that kinda gets old after a while. What about you, Goldy, why did you leave?

GOLDY LOCKS: You know, I was getting just a little sick and tired of always being cast as that dumb blonde who can't do anything else but wander through some stupid forest waiting for some stupid bears to leave their stupid house so I can break in and eat their stupid cold cereal. The writer was probably some guy who thinks that blondes have nothing better to do with their time than skip around the forest all day long and eat stale oatmeal. What do you think, Sleep?

SLEEP N. BEAUTY: (*sarcastically*) Gosh, I sure had some exciting story lines. After all, I got to wander through the Enchanted Forest and eat a poisoned piece of fruit (probably from the school cafeteria) and fall asleep for 20 years and be awakened by a dashing young dude on his big white horse who gets to plant a big wet one on my lips to wake me up and carry me away to his overpriced castle in the suburbs. (*indignantly*) Yeah, like I've got nothing better to do with my time than have some jerk with bad breath try and kiss me and tell me he can make me the happiest woman in town! Yeah, right! I mean, let's get real here! Who says I need a man, anyway? After you marry them, all they do is just sit around the castle drinking ale and burping and expecting you to clean up after them all day long. So I decided to check out and open up my own business in the city. I'm not getting any younger, you know! Hey, what about you, Snow?

SNOW WHITE: I'm sure you heard about all the things I had to do in my story. Who the heck do those writers think they are, making me live with a bunch of real short men who think that the only thing I'm good at is picking up their dirty socks and sweeping their filthy pigsty of a house? Like I really enjoy spending my days sweeping and dusting and vacuuming and washing till these guys come home so I can cook them some barbecued chicken and homemade pumpkin pie. Yeah, where is it written that the only thing we women are capable of doing is cleaning up after a bunch of slobs who track mud all over the floor and burp at dinnertime? I've certainly got better things to do than be a housemaid for seven jerks with bad manners. It didn't take too long before I just got sick and tired of the whole mess, packed my bags, and moved to Miami Beach, where I bought an apartment building for over-the-hill kings and princes. Now I'm really making some big bucks! Hey, Rapunzel, tell me, when did you decide to check out of the storybook scene?

Possible Conclusions

1. Rapunzel tells how she opened up a chain of beauty parlors and began marketing her own line of hair care products.

2. Red Riding Hood goes to work for the National Park Service and is put in charge of reintroducing wolves back into Yellowstone National Park.

3. All the characters fire the male authors of their stories, open up their own publishing company, get female writers, and publish feminist versions of their life stories.

4. One word: Hollywood.

5. Your idea.

The Unbelievable Incident in Mothergoosetown

STAGING: The narrator should be standing near the front center of the staging area. The other characters can be standing or can be sitting on tall stools.

Reporter I   Mike Raphone
X   X

Sergeant Copper
X

Mary Mary
X

Narrator
X

NARRATOR: Once upon a time there were these three bears who . . .

REPORTER I: (*interrupting*) Excuse me, buddy. But this just came in. We take you now to a wall just outside of town where our correspondent, Mike Raphone, is standing by. Come in, Mike.

MIKE RAPHONE: Thanks. We're standing here by this large and long wall that just happens to be on the outskirts of town. No one knows why it's here, but it's the site of one of the most gruesome scenes I've ever experienced in my 24 years in

131

	this business. Let's talk to Sergeant Copper of the City Police for an update. Tell us, Sergeant, what exactly happened here?
SERGEANT COPPER:	Well, it seems as though this big round guy, name of Humpty Dumpty, just climbed to the top of the wall and threatened to jump off. He just sat there and kept yelling, "The yolk's on you, Copper, the yolk's on you!"
MIKE RAPHONE:	What do you think he meant?
SERGEANT COPPER:	Well, we have all our key people working on it right now. But that's not the worst of it. You see just as he was sitting there . . . we're not sure how it happened . . . maybe it was just a gust of wind or he just lost his balance . . .
MIKE RAPHONE:	Well, what was it?
SERGEANT COPPER:	Well, for some unknown reason, he just fell off the wall and splattered all over the sidewalk. I mean, his brains were scrambled all over the place, runny stuff just poured out of him, and there were shell fragments scattered in all directions.
REPORTER I:	(*excited*) Mike, we're going to have to break away. This just came into the newsroom. It seems as though the police have just discovered something new. We take you now, live, to Mary Mary, who is standing by with the latest. Come in Mary.

Possible Conclusions

1. The police discover that the three little pigs came over from their story just to have a little fun in someone else's story.

2. While everyone was at the scene of Humpty Dumpty's jump, Cinderella, Rapunzel, Snow White, Goldilocks, and Sleeping Beauty robbed the city bank.

3. All the king's horses and all the king's men took the wrong exit off the freeway and wound up at Disneyland instead of working on piecing poor Humpty together again.

4. The "jump" never happened—it was just a clever opening for a new TV cooking program entitled "EGGS-cellent Recipes."

5. Your idea.

King Midas: In the Beginning

STAGING: There is no narrator for this story. The characters can sit on stools or walk around the staging area during the story.

Writer 1	Writer 2	Writer 3	Writer 4
X	X	X	X

WRITER 1:   O.K. guys, we've got to write another story.

WRITER 2:   Yeah, let's get started. Anyone got any good ideas?

WRITER 3:   Well, how about a story with a princess and a wicked witch and a handsome prince?

WRITER 4:   No. That's been done already. What about a beautiful maiden who lets people climb up and down her hair?

WRITER 1:   That's been done, too. Maybe we could write a story about three pigs and a wolf with an asthma problem.

WRITER 2:   No, that's been done, too. Hey, I've got it—a story about a tortoise and a hare that enter the Ironman Triathlon.

WRITER 3:   Nah, somebody did that already.

WRITER 4:   Boy, we are stuck. We've got to come up with something original and it looks like we're fresh out of ideas.

WRITER 1:   Hummmmmm. Ponder, ponder, ponder.

WRITER 2:   Hummmmmm. Ponder, ponder, ponder.

WRITER 3:   Hummmmmm. Ponder, ponder, ponder.

WRITER 4:   Hummmmmm. Ponder, ponder, ponder.

WRITER 1:   Hey, maybe I've got it. Let's write about some dude who has a magic power.

WRITER 2:   What kind of power shall we give him?

WRITER 3:   Why don't we give him the power to make animals talk?

WRITER 4:   No, that idea has been taken by a writer in another story.

WRITER 1:   Well, why don't we give him the power to disappear?

WRITER 2:   No, that's not very original. He needs to be able to do something really exciting.

WRITER 3:   Hmmmmm. How 'bout if we give him the power to change something into something else?

WRITER 4:   You mean, like change a teacher into a frog?

WRITER 3:   Well, something like that.

WRITER 1:   Gosh, now all we have to do is think of something really neat that he can change things into.

WRITER 2:   (*excitedly*) I've got it. What if everything he touches turns into salami?

WRITER 3:   (*very excited*) No, what if everything he touches turns into the latest Nintendo® game?

WRITER 4:   (*extremely excited*) No, what if everything he touches turns into . . . ?

Possible Conclusions

1. The king opens up a national chain of muffler shops and makes a ton of money.

2. The writers turn to members of the audience for their suggestions and ideas.

3. King Midas shows up at the door of the writers' house and makes an incredible and unbelievable suggestion.

4. King Midas gets tired of waiting around for the writers to make up their minds and decides to go over to another story.

5. Your idea.

Jack and Jill Don't Like the Stupid Author Who Wrote Their Story

STAGING: The narrator is seated on a tall stool. The characters can be standing or seated on tall stools.

```
                              Jack          Jill
                               X             X


           Narrator
              X
```

NARRATOR:	Once upon a time there were these two kids, Jack and Jill. They would spend all day going up this hill, but they never understood why. They never knew what they were supposed to do. (I guess they never read the original story.) Let's listen in on one of their conversations.
JILL:	Hey, Jack. Do you know this is the tenth time we've gone up this hill today? I still don't understand why the stupid author has us going up this stupid hill.
JACK:	Yeah. I don't understand either. Are we supposed to see something at the top of the hill? Are we supposed to get something at the top of the hill? Are we supposed to do something at the top of the hill? I just don't get it!

JILL:	Well, as I see it, the author wants us to go up the hill, do something at the top of the hill, and then come back down to the bottom of the hill. I don't know about you, but that sounds like the stupidest thing I've ever heard. I'm sure getting sick and tired of this stupid stupid hill!
JACK:	I don't think it's the hill that's stupid; I think the author is stupid. Who would write a story about two kids going up and down a hill all day for no reason at all! Where's the excitement? Where's the mystery?
JILL:	Yeah, you're right. This story is nothing like the fairy tales and Mother Goose rhymes that kids always read. Those stories have kids exploring deep dark forests filled with evil stepmothers and other weird creatures that eat little children. Or they get to explore mysterious castles filled with fire-breathing dragons or enchanted princes. Or they get to talk with animals that speak perfect English. And, of course, they all have happy endings.
JACK:	Like you said, the author who wrote this story sure must be stupid. He didn't even put a dragon, or a big bad wolf, or an evil giant at the top of the hill.
JILL:	Maybe we should get another author for this story. Someone who can make this a really exciting story.

Possible Conclusions

1. Jack and Jill find a really bright author who spices up their story by having them battle an enormous shark who has eaten up all the other Mother Goose characters. (You won't believe what the shark did with Hansel and Gretel!)

2. Jack and Jill get an agent, fly to California, and make tons of money in an action adventure movie.

3. Jill gets tired of always hanging around with Jack and decides to move across town and get a real job.

4. Jack and Jill get a loan from the bank and build an amusement park at the top of the hill.

5. Your idea.

Part V

THIS IS THE APPENDIX PART OF THE BOOK OR THE SECTION WHERE THOSE "BRAND X" AUTHORS PUT LOTS OF DUMB STUFF SO THAT THEIR BOOKS LOOK A LOT BIGGER THAN THEY REALLY ARE—BUT IN THIS BOOK THE STUFF HERE IS REALLY NEAT (TRUST ME)

WONDERFUL AND DELIGHTFUL TEACHER:	Wow, is this a cool book or what?
SOMEWHAT BALDING AUTHOR:	Why, thank you, oh Wonderful and Delightful Teacher. I'm glad you and your students have enjoyed all the readers theatre scripts in this book.
CREATIVE AND DYNAMIC TEACHER:	Yes, my students haven't stopped laughing for weeks. They are so "into" readers theatre. This book has really energized my entire language arts program.
SOMEWHAT BALDING AUTHOR:	Thanks. I really appreciate all your kind words and the ways in which you have been using readers theatre in your classrooms. That's the kind of stuff that authors love to hear.
GREAT AND MAGNIFICENT EDITOR:	But, oh Balding One, don't forget that the book isn't finished yet. With all these teachers excited about using readers theatre in their classrooms, you'll need to give them some additional ideas and resources so that they can continue with this magic throughout the entire year.
SOMEWHAT BALDING AUTHOR:	You, know, you're absolutely right, oh Great and Magnificent Editor. I guess that's why they pay you the big bucks!
SUAVE AND DEBONAIR TEACHER:	She's right, you know. We would like to have some stuff that will keep the excitement and energy flowing in our classrooms. We'd like to make readers theatre a permanent part of our language arts program.
SOMEWHAT BALDING AUTHOR:	Oh, I see. So, what you'd like to have is an Appendix section filled with lists of books and stories to share with your students, some weird and wacky story titles so that students can write their own readers theatre scripts, and a listing of professional resources and Web sites that will give you tons of additional ideas on using readers theatre.

PROSPECTIVE TEACHER OF THE YEAR: WOW! You are one incredible author! That's exactly what we would like to have in this part of the book. If you could do that you would have the most complete and most perfect book in the world. That would be totally awesome!

GREAT AND MAGNIFICENT EDITOR: So, what do you say, Somewhat Balding Author?

SOMEWHAT BALDING AUTHOR: Consider it done! In fact, if you turn the page right now you'll find just what you're looking for in the three appendixes. I hope you'll find these lists to be perfect extensions for using readers theatre in your classroom.

INNOCENT BYSTANDER: And so it was that all the teachers across the land used the following lists to enhance and expand the use of readers theatre in their classrooms. And they all lived happily ever after.

Appendix A: This Is a Super Cool Bibliography of Stories and Tales and Legends and Folklore and Other Great Stuff You Can Share with Your Students After They Have Performed the Scripts in This Book

Aesop. *Aesop's Fables*. New York: Viking, 1981.

Alderson, Brian, ed. *Cakes and Custard: Children's Rhymes*. New York: Morrow, 1975.

Anderson, Hans Christian. *Thumbelina*. New York: Dial, 1979.

————. *The Ugly Duckling*. New York: Harcourt Brace Jovanovich, 1979.

Asbjørnsen, Peter Christian, and Jorgen E. Moe. *Three Billy Goats Gruff*. New York: Clarion, 1981.

Brett, Jan. *Beauty and the Beast*. New York: Clarion, 1989.

————. *Goldilocks and the Three Bears*. New York: Dodd, Mead, 1987.

Briggs, Raymond. *The Mother Goose Treasury*. New York: Coward-McCann, 1966.

Brooke, William. *A Telling of the Tales*. New York: Harper & Row, 1990.

Cauley, Lorinda Bryan. *Goldilocks and the Three Bears*. New York: Putnam, 1981.

————. *The Town Mouse and the Country Mouse*. New York: Putnam, 1984.

Cohn, Amy. *From Sea to Shining Sea: A Treasury of American Folklore and Folk Songs*. New York: Scholastic, 1993.

Cole, Joanna, and Stephanie Calmenson. *Miss Mary Mac: And Other Children's Street Rhymes*. New York: Morrow, 1990.

Craig, Helen. *The Town Mouse and the Country Mouse*. Watertown, MA: Candlewick, 1992.

De Beaumont, Madame Le Prince. *Beauty and the Beast*. New York: Crown, 1986.

dePaola, Tomie. *The Comic Adventures of Old Mother Hubbard and Her Dog*. San Diego: Harcourt Brace Jovanovich, 1981.

————. *Tomie dePaola's Favorite Nursery Tales*. New York: Putnam, 1986.

————. *Tomie dePaola's Mother Goose*. New York: Putnam, 1985.

De Regniers, Beatrice Schenk. *Red Riding Hood: Retold in Verse*. New York: Atheneum, 1977.

Domanska, Janina. *Little Red Hen*. New York: Macmillan, 1973.

Edens, Cooper, ed. *The Glorious Mother Goose*. New York: Atheneum, 1988.

Ehrlich, Amy. *Random House Book of Fairy Tales*. New York: Random, 1985.

Emberley, Barbara. *The Story of Paul Bunyan*. Englewood Cliffs, NJ: Prentice-Hall, 1963.

Evslin, Bernard. *Hercules*. New York: Morrow, 1984.

Fisher, Leonard Everett. *The Olympians: Great Gods and Goddesses of Ancient Greece*. New York: Holiday, 1984.

French, Fiona. *Snow White in New York*. New York: Oxford, 1987.

Galdone, Paul. *Cinderella*. New York: McGraw-Hill, 1978.

———. *The Gingerbread Boy*. New York: Clarion, 1983.

———. *The Hare and the Tortoise*. New York: McGraw-Hill, 1962.

———. *Henny Penny*. New York: Clarion, 1984.

———. *Jack and the Beanstalk*. New York: Clarion, 1982.

———. *Little Bo-Peep*. New York: Clarion, 1982.

———. *The Little Red Hen*. New York: McGraw-Hill, 1985.

———. *Little Red Riding Hood*. New York: McGraw-Hill, 1974.

———. *The Magic Porridge Pot*. New York: Clarion, 1976.

———. *Old Mother Hubbard and Her Dog*. New York: McGraw-Hill, 1960.

———. *Rumplestiltskin*. New York: Clarion, 1985.

———. *Three Aesop Fox Fables*. New York: Clarion, 1971.

———. *The Three Bears*. New York: Clarion, 1985.

———. *Three Little Kittens*. New York: Clarion, 1986.

———. *The Three Little Pigs*. New York: Clarion, 1984.

Goode, Diane. *Diane Goode's Book of Silly Stories and Songs*. New York: Dutton, 1992.

Greenaway, Kate. *Mother Goose: Or, the Old Nursery Rhymes*. New York: Warne, 1981.

Griego, Morgot C., Betsy L. Bucks, Sharon S. Gilbert, and Laurel H. Kimball. *Tortillas Para Mama and Other Spanish Nursery Rhymes*. New York: Holt, Rinehart & Winston, 1981.

Grimm, Jakob, and Wilhelm Grimm. *The Bremen Town Musicians*. New York: Harper & Row, 1987.

———. *Cinderella*. New York: Greenwillow, 1981.

———. *The Donkey Prince*. New York: Doubleday, 1977.

———. *The Elves and the Shoemaker*. Chicago: Follett, 1967.

———. *Favorite Tales from Grimm*. New York: Four Winds, 1982.

———. *The Frog Prince*. New York: Scholastic, 1987.

———. *Grimm's Fairy Tales: Twenty Stories Illustrated by Arthur Rackham*. New York: Viking, 1973.

———. *Hansel and Gretel*. New York: Morrow, 1980.

———. *Little Red Riding Hood*. New York: Atheneum, 1988.

———. *Popular Folk Tales: The Brothers Grimm*. New York: Doubleday, 1978.

———. *Rapunzel*. New York: Holiday House, 1987.

———. *Rumplestiltskin*. New York: Four Winds, 1973.

———. *The Shoemaker and the Elves*. New York: Lothrop, 1983.

————. *The Sleeping Beauty*. New York: Atheneum, 1979.

————. *Snow White*. Boston: Little, Brown, 1974.

————. *Snow White and Rose Red*. New York: Delacorte, 1965.

————. *Snow White and the Seven Dwarfs*. New York: Farrar, 1987.

————. *Tom Thumb*. New York: Walck, 1974.

Hale, Sara. *Mary Had a Little Lamb*. New York: Holiday House, 1984.

Haley, Gail. *Jack and the Bean Tree*. New York: Crown, 1986.

Harper, Wilhelmina. *The Gunniwolf*. New York: Dutton, 1967.

Hayes, Sarah. *Bad Egg: The True Story of Humpty Dumpty*. Boston: Little, Brown, 1987.

Hague, Michael, ed. *Mother Goose*. New York: Holt, Rinehart & Winston, 1984.

Hastings, Selina. *Sir Gawain and the Loathly Lady*. New York: Lothrop, Lee & Shepard, 1985.

Hodges, Margaret. *Saint George and the Dragon*. Boston: Little, Brown, 1984.

Huck, Charlotte. *Princess Furball*. New York: Greenwillow, 1989.

Hutton, Warwick. *Beauty and the Beast*. New York: Atheneum, 1985.

Hutchinson, Veronica S. *Henny Penny*. Boston: Little, Brown, 1976.

Ivimey, John W. *The Complete Story of The Three Blind Mice*. New York: Clarion, 1987.

Jacobs, Joseph. *Jack and the Beanstalk*. New York: Putnam's, 1983.

————. *The Three Little Pigs*. New York: Atheneum, 1980.

Jeffers, Susan. *If Wishes Were Horses: Mother Goose Rhymes*. New York: Dutton, 1979.

Kellogg, Steven. *Chicken Little*. New York: Morrow, 1985.

————. *Johnny Appleseed*. New York: Morrow, 1988.

————. *Mike Fink*. New York: Morrow, 1992.

————. *Paul Bunyan*. New York: Morrow, 1974.

————. *Pecos Bill*. New York: Morrow, 1986.

Kimmel, Eric. *The Gingerbread Man*. New York: Holiday, 1993.

Kingsley, Charles. *The Heroes*. New York: Mayflower, 1980.

Lobel, Arnold. *Gregory Griggs and Other Nursery Rhyme People*. New York: Greenwillow, 1978

————. *The Random House Book of Mother Goose*. New York: Random House, 1986.

Marshall, James. *Goldilocks and the Three Bears*. New York: Dial, 1988.

————. *Hansel and Gretel*. New York: Dial, 1990.

————. *James Marshall's Mother Goose*. New York: Farrar, Straus & Giroux, 1979.

————. *Red Riding Hood*. New York: Dial, 1987.

Martin, Sarah. *The Comic Adventures of Old Mother Hubbard and Her Dog*. San Diego: Harcourt Brace, 1981.

McKinley, Robin. *The Outlaws of Sherwood*. New York: Greenwillow, 1988.

Miles, Bernard. *Robin Hood: His Life and Legend*. New York: Hamlyn, 1979.

Miller, Mitchell. *One Misty Moisty Morning*. New York: Farrar, Straus & Giroux, 1971.

Newbery, John. *The Original Mother Goose's Melody*. New York: Gale, 1969.

Opie, Iona, and Peter Opie. *A Nursery Companion*. London: Oxford University Press, 1980.

———. *The Oxford Nursery Rhyme Book*. London: Oxford University Press, 1984.

———. *Tail Feathers from Mother Goose: The Opie Rhyme Book*. Boston: Little, Brown, 1988.

Ormerod, Jan. *The Story of Chicken Licken*. New York: Lothrop, 1986.

Oxenbury, Helen. *The Helen Oxenbury Nursery Story Book*. New York: Knopf, 1985.

Pearson, Tracey. *Old MacDonald Had a Farm*. New York: Dial, 1984.

Perrault, Charles. *Cinderella*. New York: Dial, 1985.

———. *Little Red Riding Hood*. New York: Scholastic, 1971.

———. *Puss in Boots*. New York: Clarion, 1976.

———. *The Sleeping Beauty*. New York: Viking, 1972.

Provensen, Alice, and Martin Provensen. *Old Mother Hubbard*. New York: Random House, 1982.

Riordan, James. *Tales of King Arthur*. New York: Rand McNally, 1982.

Rounds, Glen. *Old MacDonald Has a Farm*. New York: Holiday House, 1989.

———. *Three Little Pigs and the Big Bad Wolf*. New York: Holiday, 1992.

Scieszka, Jon. *The Stinky Cheese Man and Other Fairly Stupid Tales*. New York: Viking, 1992.

———. *The True Story of the 3 Little Pigs*. New York: Viking, 1989.

Southey, Robert. *The Three Bears*. New York: Putnam, 1984.

Spier, Peter. *London Bridge Is Falling Down*. New York: Doubleday, 1967.

Stevens, Janet. *Goldilocks and the Three Bears*. New York: Holiday House, 1986.

———. *The House That Jack Built*. New York: Holiday House, 1985.

———. *The Tortoise and the Hare*. New York: Holiday House, 1984.

———. *The Town Mouse and the Country Mouse*. New York: Holiday House, 1987.

Still, James. *Jack and the Wonder Beans*. New York: Putnam, 1977.

Stoutenburg, Adrien. *American Tall Tales*. New York: Viking, 1966.

Tarrant, Margaret. *Nursery Rhymes*. New York: Crowell, 1978.

Thompson, Pat, ed. *Rhymes Around the Day*. New York: Lothrop, Lee & Shepard, 1983.

Tripp, Wallace. *Granfa' Grig Had a Pig and Other Rhymes Without Reason from Mother Goose.* Boston: Little, Brown, 1976.

Tudor, Tasha. *Mother Goose.* New York: Walck, 1972.

Watson, Wendy. *Wendy Watson's Mother Goose.* New York: Lothrop, Lee & Shepard, 1989.

Watts, Bernadette. *Goldilocks and the Three Bears.* New York: Holt, Rinehart & Winston, 1985.

Wildsmith, Brian. *Brian Wildsmith's Mother Goose.* New York: Oxford University Press, 1982.

Willard, Nancy. *Beauty and the Beast.* New York: Harcourt Brace Jovanovich, 1992.

Zemach, Harve. *Duffy and the Devil.* New York: Farrar, Straus & Giroux, 1973.

Zuromskis, Diane. *The Farmer in the Dell.* Boston: Little, Brown, 1978.

Appendix B: Hold on to Your Hat, Because Here's the Part of the Book Where You'll Discover Some Weird Stuff to Share with Your Students Throughout the Year

Well, being a highly intelligent and exceedingly bright person, you've probably noticed that we're getting near the end of this book (groan, sigh; groan, sigh). That usually means that the author has run out of ideas or has some other things that he needs to do at this point in his life (such as vacuum the living room, paint the shutters on his house, or some other tasks that keep showing up on his "honey-do" list). Well, that may be the case in all those "Brand X" books written by all those "Brand X" authors—but not in this book. Because, even though we are getting close to the last couple of pages in this book, we aren't finished with all the wonderfully creative and highly engaging stuff you've come to expect in this book. (I think it's safe to say that I'd rather be writing these ideas than scrubbing the bathroom or doing those things on the "honey-do" list.)

So, you're probably wondering what this wild and wacky author has in store for you at this point in the book. That's right—you guessed it—some more readers theatre ideas. Except this time, the ideas aren't in the form of full scripts or partial scripts, but rather are potential script titles that you can share with your students so that they will be suitably "energized" and will want to write their own readers theatre scripts from scratch to share with their classmates and other students in the school. "How does this work?" you may be asking. "Very simply," I might reply.

Share one or more of the script titles below with your students. Invite them to create their own readers theatre scripts using the suggested titles along with their own characters, dialogue, action, and scenes. I have found it advantageous to divide my class into several small groups and invite each group to select one of the titles below. Each group is then encouraged to develop their own script, which can be shared with the remainder of the class at a later time.

These titles, however, should only serve as starting points for your students. After you've shared some of the original stories (see Appendix A) with your class, invite students to generate their own weird and wacky titles and the accompanying weird and wacky scripts. What you will discover is not only students who are immersed in the creativity of readers theatre, but students who are provided with authentic opportunities to use their language arts in meaningful and productive contexts.

So, even though we're pretty close to the end of the book, you've got some more really neat ideas you can share with your students. (Now, aren't you glad you kept reading this book?)

1. The Ugly Duckling Turns into the Pretty Good-Looking Duckling and Then Enters a Beauty Pageant

2. Don't Shake King Midas's Hand or You'll Be Sorry

3. The Three Little Pigs Blow Down the Wolf's House

4. Paul Bunyan Is Just Some Big Guy with an Overweight Ox

5. The Gingerbread Man Gets Baked at 350° for 20 to 25 Minutes

6. "Cinderella —Get A Life!"

7. Chicken Little Is Found at the Local KFC Restaurant (and It's Not a Pretty Sight!)

8. Mary Had a Little Lamb That Grew up to Become a Big Bad Sheep with an Attitude Problem

9. The Three Bears Move into the Neighborhood and Then Something Really Scary Happens

10. Mother Goose Is Really a Duck in Disguise

11. Please Don't Kiss Me —I'm Just a Frog!

12. Hey, What's the Deal with This Fire-Breathing Dragon Hanging Around the School?

13. Snow White Gets an Agent and Changes Her Name to _____.

14. Johnny Appleseed Wanders All over the Map and Eventually Winds up in Cleveland

15. Check It Out! Rip Van Winkle Snores Like a Pig

16. John Henry Was a Wimp (Sort Of)

17. King Arthur Was a Wimp (Sort Of)

18. Robin Hood Was a Wimp (Sort Of)

19. Hey, Here's a Story That's Full of Wimps (Sort Of)

20. We Didn't Know What to Title This Story So We Just Put All These Words at the Top of the Page

21. Another Story Without a Title (Trust Us, It's Really Good)

22. The Fairy Godmother Gets a Ticket for Flying Too Fast

23. A Story About Mike Fink (and Who the Heck Was Mike Fink, Anyway?)

24. A Story That Didn't Take Place in "Once Upon a Time" Time

25. Salamanders (That's It —A Whole Story Just about Salamanders)

26. The Big Bad Wolf and the Evil Stepmother Join a Motorcycle Gang

27. Hercules Is Not As Strong As He Thinks He Is

28. The Author of *Silly Salamanders and Other Slightly Stupid Stuff for Readers Theatre* Has a Secret Desire to Be a Rock and Roll Singer

29. Our Teacher Has a Secret Desire to Be a Rock and Roll Singer

30. Our Teacher Is the Most Beautiful and Most Intelligent Person on the Entire Planet

31. Rapunzel Goes Bald (Oh No, Oh No)

32. Goldilocks Goes Bald (Oh No, Oh No)

33. Sleeping Beauty Goes Bald (Oh No, Oh No)

34. Hey, What's Happening Here? Everybody's Going Bald.

35. Cinderella, Snow White, and Sleeping Beauty Start a New Business (and They Don't Hire Any Men)

36. Goldilocks Is Arrested for Breaking and Entering the Three Bears' House

37. Paul Bunyan Makes a Big Hole in the Ground (Also Known As the Grand Canyon)

38. Hey, There's a Dragon in Our Classroom!

39. William Tell Tries to Shoot an Apple off His Son's Head —Except His Aim Isn't Very Good

40. Pecos Bill and the Salamander (Hey, What's Pecos Bill Doing Riding a Salamander?)

41. The Smartest Class in the Whole World (This Isn't a Fairy Tale)

42. Your Idea

Appendix C: Some Resources and Other Stuff That Authors Always Put at the End of Their Books in Case You Want to Check Out Some Additional Materials About the Topic of the Book

Books About Readers Theatre

Braun, W., and C. Braun. *Readers Theatre: Scripted Rhymes and Rhythms.* Calgary, Canada AB: Braun & Braun Educational Enterprises Ltd., 1995.

Coger, L. I., and M. R. White. *Readers Theatre Handbook: A Dramatic Approach to Literature.* Glenview, IL: Scott, Foresman, 1982.

Dixon, N., A. Davies, and C. Politano. *Learning with Readers Theatre: Building Connections.* Winnipeg, Canada: Peguis Publishers, 1996.

Hill, S. *Readers Theatre: Performing the Text.* Armadale, Australia: Eleanor Curtain Publishing, 1990.

Johnson, T. D., and D. R. Louis. *Bringing It All Together: A Program for Literacy.* Portsmouth, NH: Heinemann, 1990.

Plant, R. *Readers Theatre in the Elementary Classroom: A Take Part Teacher's Guide.* North Vancouver, BC: Take Part Productions, 1990.

Shepard, A. *Stories on Stage: Scripts for Reader's Theater.* New York: H. W. Wilson, 1993.

Sloyer, S. *Readers Theatre: Story Dramatization in the Classroom.* Urbana, IL: National Council for Teachers of English, 1982.

Tanner, F. *Creative Communication: Projects in Acting, Speaking, Oral Reading.* Pocatello, ID: Clark Publishing Co, 1979.

———. *Readers Theatre Fundamentals.* Pocatello, ID: Clark Publishing Co., 1993.

Sources for Additional Readers Theatre Scripts

Barchers, S. *Fifty Fabulous Fables: Beginning Readers Theatre.* Englewood, CO: Teacher Ideas Press, 1997.

———. *Multicultural Folktales: Readers Theatre for Elementary Students.* Englewood, CO: Teacher Ideas Press, 2000.

———. *Readers Theatre for Beginning Readers.* Englewood, CO: Teacher Ideas Press, 1993.

———. *Scary Readers Theatre.* Englewood, CO: Teacher Ideas Press, 1994.

Criscoe, B. L., and P. J. Lanasa. *Fairy Tales for Two Readers.* Englewood, CO: Teacher Ideas Press, 1995.

Fredericks, A. D. *Frantic Frogs and Other Frankly Fractured Folktales for Readers Theatre.* Englewood, CO: Teacher Ideas Press, 1993.

———. *Tadpole Tales and Other Totally Terrific Treats for Readers Theatre.* Englewood, CO: Teacher Ideas Press, 1997.

Georges, C., and C. Cornett. *Reader's Theatre.* Buffalo, NY: D.O.K. Publishers, 1990.

Haven, K. *Great Moments in Science: Experiments and Readers Theatre*. Englewood, CO: Teacher Ideas Press, 1996.

Latrobe, K. H., and M. K. Laughlin. *Readers Theatre for Young Adults*. Englewood, CO: Teacher Ideas Press, 1989.

Latrobe, K. H., C. Casey, and L. A. Gann. *Social Studies Readers Theatre for Young Adults*. Englewood, CO: Teacher Ideas Press, 1991.

Laughlin, M. K., and K. H. Latrobe. *Readers Theatre for Children*. Englewood, CO: Teacher Ideas Press, 1990.

Laughlin, M. K., P. T. Black, and K. H. Latrobe. *Social Studies Readers Theatre for Children*. Englewood, CO: Teacher Ideas Press, 1991.

Pfeffinger, C.R. *Holiday Readers Theatre*. Englewood, CO: Teacher Ideas Press, 1994.

Web Sites

http://www.aaronshep.com/rt/index.html

How to use readers theatre, sample scripts from a children's author who specializes in readers theatre, and an extensive list of resources are included at this site.

http://falcon.jmu.edu/~ramseyil/drama.htm

Lots of links for storytelling, creative dramatics, puppetry, and readers theatre for children and young adults highlight this site.

http://mcrel.org/resources/plus/theatre.html

Includes lesson plan activities, teacher's guides, how to adapt stories to a readers theatre format, and online children's stories.

http://www.readerstheatre.com

This organization is dedicated to the development and use of readers theatre in education.

http://www.geocities.com/EnchantedForest/Tower/3235/index.html

This is a download page for the "RT Script Pack," a set of readers theatre scripts in Microsoft Word format. Reading levels vary from beginner to adult.

http://www.loiswalker.com/catalog/

Includes lots of readers theatre scripts for a variety of reading levels and ages.

http://www.storycart.com

Storycart Press's subscription service provides an inexpensive opportunity to have timely scripts delivered to teachers each month. Each script is created or adapted by well-known writer Suzanne Barchers, author of four readers theatre books (see above).

Professional Organizations

Readers Theatre International
P.O. Box 65059
North Hill, R.P.O.
Calgary, Canada AB T2N 4T6
(403) 220-1770
Toll free: 1-888-221-1770

Institute for Readers Theatre
P.O. Box 178333
San Diego, CA 92177
(619) 276-1948

O.K., here he is—that "Somewhat Balding Author" you've been reading about. Of course, you'll notice that through the use of trick photography and a clever application of expensive dye he appears to have a full head of hair (although we're firmly convinced his head is full of something else). What is equally obvious is that this guy is no enchanted prince! After all, he wears glasses, he drives a pick-up truck, and he wears a tie. (When was the last time you ever saw a prince in a tie . . . or in a pick-up truck?) True, he does have that incessant smile plastered on his face—but so do a lot of insurance salesmen and used car dealers.

Anthony D. Fredericks

Now, here's what we do know about "Somewhat Balding Author": His background includes more than 30 years of experience as a classroom teacher, reading specialist, curriculum coordinator, staff developer, author, professional storyteller, and college professor in elementary science and language arts. He is a prolific author, having written more than 50 teacher resource books on science, social studies, and language arts topics (including the wildly popular *Frantic Frogs and Other Frankly Fractured Folktales for Readers Theatre*). Additionally, he's authored two dozen highly acclaimed children's books about animals and environmental studies (e.g., *Cannibal Animals*, *Elephants for Kids*, *Exploring the Oceans*, and *Slugs*). In addition, he maintains an award-winning Web site for elementary teachers (http://www.afredericks.com) with the latest information on classroom resources.

Our "Somewhat Balding Author" currently teaches elementary methods courses at York College in York, Pennsylvania (where students have never referred to him as a prince, enchanted or otherwise). He is often found wandering through the children's section of major book stores or making friends with fire-breathing dragons, fairy godmothers, or the inevitable salamander. It should also be noted that "Somewhat Balding Author" is married to "Incredibly Ravishing Princess" and lives with "Totally Insane Cat" and "Frequently Drooling Dog."

More Readers Theatre